SORRENTO TRAVEL GUIDE

2024 Edition

Everything You Need To Know Before Visiting Sorrento. Practical Pointers, Essential Tips for a Seamless Sorrento Sojourn

Paul Patton

TABLE OF CONTENT

Important Notice Before You Continue Reading!

Step into a world beyond your imagination. This comprehensive travel guide invites you to embark on a remarkable journey through Sorrento. Brace yourself for a truly immersive experience, where your imagination, creativity, and sense of adventure will be your compass. Leave behind the glossy images and preconceived notions because we believe that genuine beauty should be encountered firsthand, untainted by visual filters. Prepare yourself for an exhilarating exploration where every monument, every place, and every hidden corner eagerly anticipate your arrival, ready to amaze and captivate you. Why spoil the thrill of that initial encounter, that overwhelming sense of awe? It's time to embrace the unparalleled excitement of becoming your own guide, where the boundaries are nonexistent, and your imagination becomes the sole means of transportation.

Unlike conventional guides, this book intentionally forgoes intricate images & maps. Why, you might wonder? Because we firmly believe that the most extraordinary discoveries transpire when you surrender to the unknown, when you allow yourself to get delightfully lost in the enigmatic charm of the surroundings. No predefined itineraries or rigid directions, for we yearn for you to immerse yourself in Sorrento on your own terms, free from boundaries or constraints. Surrender to the whims of exploration and uncover hidden treasures that no map or images could ever reveal. Dare to be bold, follow your instincts, and prepare to be astounded. The enchantment of this journey unfolds within your world, where roads materialize with each step, and the most astonishing adventures lie in the folds of the unknown. Embrace the magic that awaits you as you paint vivid images with your own eyes, for the truest and most beautiful pictures are the ones you create within your heart.

introduction

Embark on a captivating journey through the sun-kissed landscapes and rich cultural tapestry of Sorrento with our comprehensive travel guide. Nestled along the breathtaking Amalfi Coast, Sorrento beckons with its enchanting allure—a destination where ancient history meets modern charm. As you flip through the pages of this guide, envision yourself strolling down cobbled streets, indulging in delectable cuisine, and basking in the Mediterranean sun.

More than just a travel companion, this guide is your key to unlocking the secrets of Sorrento. Whether you're a seasoned traveler or a first-time explorer, we invite you to immerse yourself in the vibrant hues of Sorrento's seaside cliffs, discover hidden gems tucked away in its historic alleys, and savor the flavors that define this Italian paradise.

From the moment you open these pages, you'll find yourself captivated by the beauty that Sorrento exudes. We've meticulously curated a wealth of information to ensure that your journey is not only seamless but also enriched with the unique experiences that make Sorrento a destination like no other.

Prepare to be transported to a world where lemon groves perfume the air, azure waters stretch as far as the eye can see, and every corner holds a story waiting to be unraveled. This isn't just a travel guide—it's your ticket to a sojourn filled with enchantment, discovery, and the timeless magic of Sorrento. So, fasten your seatbelt and let the adventure begin. Sorrento awaits, and we're here to be your trusted guide on this extraordinary odyssey.

Why you should Visit

Sorrento, a charming coastal town located in southwestern Italy, is a destination that beckons travelers with its breathtaking beauty, rich history, and warm hospitality. Nestled atop cliffs that overlook the Bay of Naples, Sorrento is a place that seamlessly combines the allure of the sea with the charm of a traditional Italian town. If you're wondering why you should visit Sorrento, let me take you on a journey through the enchanting landscapes, cultural gems, and culinary delights that make this destination a must-see.

One of the primary reasons to visit Sorrento is its stunning panoramic views. Perched on the Sorrentine Peninsula, the town provides a picturesque vantage point to admire the azure waters of the Tyrrhenian Sea and the majestic Mount Vesuvius in the distance. The captivating scenery is a constant companion as you stroll through Sorrento's narrow streets, adorned with colorful bougainvillea and lined with lemon groves.

Speaking of lemons, Sorrento is renowned for its prized lemon variety, the Sfusato Amalfitano. The town's lemon groves not only add to the visual appeal but also contribute to the local economy through the production of limoncello, a famous lemon liqueur. Visitors have the opportunity to tour lemon orchards, learn about the cultivation process, and savor the distinct flavor of Sorrento's lemons in various culinary delights.

Beyond its natural beauty, Sorrento boasts a rich history that is reflected in its architecture and landmarks. The historic center is a treasure trove of medieval and Renaissance buildings, including the impressive Cathedral of Sorrento. Dating back to the 15th century, the cathedral features a striking façade and houses notable artworks, providing a glimpse into the town's artistic and religious heritage.

For history enthusiasts, a visit to the Museo Correale di Terranova is a must. This museum showcases an extensive collection of art and artifacts, offering insight into Sorrento's past and its ties to the broader Campania region. From ceramics and paintings to archaeological finds, the museum provides a comprehensive overview of the area's cultural evolution.

Sorrento's proximity to renowned archaeological sites adds another layer to its appeal. A short boat ride or drive away, visitors can explore the ancient ruins of Pompeii and Herculaneum, preserved by the ash of Mount Vesuvius's catastrophic eruption. Walking through the streets of these once-thriving Roman cities is a fascinating journey back in time, providing a stark contrast to the modern vibrancy of Sorrento.

Culinary enthusiasts will find Sorrento to be a haven for authentic Italian cuisine. The town's waterfront is dotted with seafood restaurants offering freshly caught delights, while the cobblestone streets are lined with pizzerias and trattorias serving mouthwatering local specialties. From handmade pasta dishes to fresh seafood and, of course, the delectable lemon-infused desserts, Sorrento's culinary scene is a feast for the senses.

The warmth and hospitality of the locals further enhance the Sorrento experience. The genuine friendliness of the people creates a welcoming atmosphere, making visitors feel like they're not just tourists but cherished guests. Engaging with the locals, whether in a traditional market or a family-owned restaurant, adds a personal touch to your Sorrento sojourn.

In addition to its cultural and culinary offerings, Sorrento serves as an ideal base for exploring the Amalfi Coast. Day trips to nearby Positano, Amalfi, and Ravello unveil more stunning landscapes and cultural gems, creating a well-rounded itinerary for travelers seeking a diverse and enriching experience.

Sorrento beckons with its captivating views, rich history, delectable cuisine, and warm hospitality. Whether you're a history buff, a foodie, or simply seeking a tranquil retreat by the sea, Sorrento has something to offer. This charming town is not just a destination; it's an immersive experience that leaves a lasting impression on every traveler fortunate enough to explore its enchanting streets and coastal wonders.

History & Customs

The story of Sorrento is as captivating as its breathtaking views of the Tyrrhenian Sea, and its customs are deeply rooted in the traditions of the region.

The history of Sorrento dates back to ancient times, with evidence of human settlement in the area dating as far back as the prehistoric era. The Greeks were among the first to recognize the allure of Sorrento, establishing colonies in the region around the 7th century BC. Over the centuries, Sorrento became a vital part of the Roman Empire, and its strategic location made it a sought-after territory for various rulers and conquerors.

One of the most notable aspects of Sorrento's history is its association with the Roman emperor Augustus. Legend has it that Augustus fell in love with the beauty of Sorrento and, in 29 BC, decided to build a villa overlooking the sea. The remains of this villa, known as the Villa Pollio Felice, can still be explored today, offering a glimpse into the opulence of ancient Roman life.

Throughout the medieval period, Sorrento experienced a series of conquests and dominations by different powers, including the Byzantines, Normans, and Saracens. Each of these influences left its mark on the culture and architecture of Sorrento, creating a unique blend of styles that is evident in the town's charming streets and historic buildings.

In the Renaissance era, Sorrento flourished as a center of art and culture. The town became known for its skilled artisans, producing exquisite inlaid woodwork and intricate lace. The Sorrentine Peninsula's lemons also gained fame during this time, with the cultivation of the region's renowned limoncello liqueur, a tradition that continues to thrive today.

Sorrento's customs are deeply intertwined with its history, and many of them have been passed down through generations. One such custom is the celebration of St. Antonino, the patron saint of Sorrento. Every year on February 14th, locals participate in religious processions and festivities to honor St. Antonino, seeking his blessings for the town.

The religious traditions of Sorrento extend to the annual Feast of the Assumption on August 15th, a day dedicated to the Virgin Mary. The highlight of the celebration is a colorful procession through the streets, featuring religious icons, music, and traditional attire. The Feast of the Assumption is a time for both locals and visitors to come together in a joyous celebration of faith and community.

Sorrento is also renowned for its vibrant music and dance traditions. The Tarantella, a lively and energetic folk dance, has roots in southern Italy and is often performed during festive occasions. The rhythm and movements of the Tarantella reflect the lively spirit of Sorrento and add to the town's festive atmosphere.

Culinary customs play a significant role in Sorrento's identity, with the region's cuisine celebrated for its fresh and flavorful ingredients. Seafood, lemons, and olive oil are staples in Sorrentine dishes, reflecting the town's coastal location and fertile land. Visitors can indulge in local specialties such as Gnocchi alla Sorrentina, a potato-based pasta dish, and enjoy the citrusy delights of limoncello after a satisfying meal.

In addition to its historical and cultural richness, Sorrento continues to attract visitors with its stunning landscapes and world-class hospitality. The town's iconic cliffs, dotted with colorful buildings and lush gardens, provide a breathtaking backdrop for exploration. Whether strolling through the narrow streets of the historic center, savoring local delicacies, or simply enjoying the panoramic views of the Mediterranean, visitors to Sorrento are immersed in a captivating blend of history, tradition, and natural beauty.

Sorrento's history and customs weave a tapestry of stories and traditions that have shaped the town into the enchanting destination it is today. From its ancient Roman roots to the vibrant celebrations of saints and the lively music and dance traditions, Sorrento invites travelers to step back in time while savoring the timeless beauty of the Amalfi Coast. Whether exploring archaeological wonders, participating in local festivities, or savoring the flavors of Sorrentine cuisine, visitors are sure to be captivated by the history and customs that make Sorrento a truly magical destination.

Chapter 1: Planning Your Trip

Best time to visit

Choosing the best time to visit Sorrento depends on your preferences, as each season brings its own unique charm to this coastal paradise.

One of the most popular times to visit Sorrento is during the spring months of April to June. During this period, the weather is mild and pleasant, with temperatures ranging from 15 to 25 degrees Celsius (59 to 77 degrees Fahrenheit). The vibrant colors of blooming flowers and lush landscapes create a breathtaking backdrop for exploring the town and its surroundings. Spring is also an ideal time for outdoor activities, such as hiking along the scenic trails of the Amalfi Coast or taking a boat tour to the enchanting island of Capri.

As the summer sun begins to shine, Sorrento transforms into a bustling hub of energy and excitement. The months of July and August mark the peak of the tourist season, attracting visitors from around the world. The Mediterranean climate ensures warm temperatures, with highs reaching 30 degrees Celsius (86 degrees Fahrenheit) or more. Summer is perfect for indulging in Sorrento's famous lemon-infused dishes, lounging on the beaches, and sipping refreshing limoncello while enjoying panoramic sea views. However, be prepared for larger crowds and higher prices during this peak season.

For those seeking a more relaxed and budget-friendly experience, the fall season from September to November offers a delightful alternative. The weather remains pleasant, with temperatures ranging from 18 to 25 degrees Celsius (64 to 77 degrees Fahrenheit). The summer crowds start to dissipate, allowing you to explore Sorrento's attractions, such as the historic Piazza Tasso and the 15th-century cathedral, without the hustle and bustle. Fall also brings the harvest season, providing a chance to taste fresh, locally produced wines and indulge in the region's culinary delights.

While winter may not be the traditional choice for a Sorrento visit, it has its own unique appeal. From December to February, the town takes on a quieter and more intimate atmosphere. While the temperatures are cooler, ranging from 8 to 15 degrees Celsius (46 to 59 degrees Fahrenheit), Sorrento's charm shines through its festive decorations and holiday spirit. Winter is an excellent time to experience the local culture, savor traditional winter dishes, and enjoy the solitude of the coastal landscapes.

Regardless of the season you choose, Sorrento's allure lies in its timeless beauty and the warmth of its people. To make the most of your visit, consider the type of experience you desire. If you prefer vibrant energy and bustling streets, summer might be your ideal time. For a more intimate and budget-friendly escape, fall or winter could be the perfect fit. Whatever the season, Sorrento welcomes you with open arms, promising an unforgettable journey through its captivating landscapes and rich cultural heritage.

Visa and Travel Requirements

Before you embark on your journey to this enchanting coastal town in Italy, it's essential to be well-informed about the visa and travel requirements to ensure a smooth and enjoyable experience.

Visa Requirements:

Italy is a member of the Schengen Area, which means that citizens of certain countries can enter Italy and other

Schengen countries without a visa for short stays. However, it's crucial to check whether your country is on the list of visa-exempt nations or if you need to obtain a Schengen visa.

If you are a citizen of a Schengen Area country, you can enter Italy for up to 90 days within a 180-day period without a visa. Citizens of non-Schengen countries may need to apply for a Schengen visa at the Italian embassy or consulate in their home country before traveling to Sorrento.

Ensure that your passport is valid for at least three months beyond your planned departure date from the Schengen Area. It's also advisable to have travel insurance that covers medical expenses and emergency repatriation.

Travel Planning:

Once you've sorted out the visa requirements, it's time to plan the logistics of your journey to Sorrento. The nearest international airport is Naples International Airport (NAP), which is well-connected to major cities in Europe and other continents.

From the airport, you can reach Sorrento by various transportation options, including trains, buses, and private transfers. The Circumvesuviana train is a popular choice, providing a scenic route from Naples to Sorrento. Alternatively, you can hire a private car service or take a bus, offering flexibility and comfort.

Currency and Money Matters:

Italy uses the Euro (EUR) as its official currency. It's advisable to carry some euros in cash for small purchases, especially in local markets. Credit cards are widely accepted in Sorrento, but it's always a good idea to notify your bank about your travel dates to avoid any issues with card transactions.

ATMs are readily available in Sorrento, allowing you to withdraw cash as needed. Be aware of any foreign transaction fees that your bank may charge, and consider obtaining a travel money card for added convenience.

Local Customs and Etiquette:

While Sorrento is a tourist-friendly destination, it's essential to be aware of local customs and etiquette. Italians value politeness and respect, so a friendly "buongiorno" (good morning) or "grazie" (thank you) goes a long way.

Dress modestly when visiting religious sites, and keep in mind that it's customary to greet people with a kiss on both cheeks in social situations. Tipping is generally appreciated but not mandatory, as a service charge is often included in restaurant bills.

Health and Safety:

Sorrento is known for its safe and welcoming atmosphere, but it's crucial to prioritize your health and safety during your visit. Italy has an excellent healthcare system, but it's advisable to have travel insurance that covers medical emergencies.

Ensure that your routine vaccinations are up to date, and consider getting travel vaccinations based on the duration and nature of your stay. It's also wise to carry any necessary medications and have a basic understanding of the local emergency services.

Language and Communication:

Italian is the official language in Sorrento, but English is widely spoken in tourist areas. Learning a few basic Italian phrases can enhance your travel experience and endear you to the locals. Most signage, especially in tourist spots, is also available in English.

Having a translation app on your phone can be helpful, and it's always a good idea to carry a small phrasebook for situations where English may not be readily understood.

Exploring Sorrento:

Sorrento offers a plethora of attractions, from the historic Piazza Tasso to the stunning Amalfi Coast. Plan your itinerary to include visits to iconic landmarks such as the Sorrento Cathedral, Villa Comunale, and the Marina Grande.

Indulge in the local cuisine, known for its fresh seafood, delicious pasta, and refreshing limoncello. Explore the narrow streets filled with boutique shops, and don't forget to take in the panoramic views of the Gulf of Naples.

Consider taking day trips to nearby attractions, including the ruins of Pompeii and Herculaneum, the island of Capri, and the Amalfi Coast. Each of these destinations adds a unique flavor to your Sorrento experience.

Visiting Sorrento is a journey filled with cultural richness, natural beauty, and culinary delights. By understanding and planning for the visa and travel requirements, you can make the most of your time in this idyllic Italian destination. From the moment you arrive at Naples International Airport to the exploration of Sorrento's charming streets, every step of your journey is sure to be a memorable experience.

What to pack

When planning a visit to Sorrento, a picturesque town on the Amalfi Coast in Italy, it's essential to pack wisely to ensure a comfortable and enjoyable experience. Here's a guide on what to pack for your Sorrento adventure.

1. Comfortable Footwear:

Sorrento's streets are charmingly narrow and winding, often made of cobblestone. A pair of comfortable walking shoes is a must to navigate these streets and explore the town comfortably. Whether you're strolling through the historic center or venturing down to the marina, comfortable footwear will make your explorations much more enjoyable.

2. Light and Breathable Clothing:

The Mediterranean climate in Sorrento can be warm, especially during the summer months. Pack lightweight and breathable clothing to stay cool as you explore the town and its surroundings. Consider bringing a hat and sunglasses for added sun protection, especially if you plan on spending time at the beach.

3. Swimwear:

Sorrento boasts beautiful beaches and crystal-clear waters. Don't forget to pack your swimwear, whether you plan to relax on the beach or take a refreshing dip in the Tyrrhenian Sea. Many hotels also have pools, so a swimsuit is a versatile addition to your packing list.

4. Power Adapter:

Italy uses the Europlug Type C and Type F electrical outlets. Make sure to pack a suitable power adapter to keep your devices charged and ready for capturing the stunning landscapes and moments in Sorrento.

5. Camera and Binoculars:
Sorrento offers breathtaking panoramic views, especially from high vantage points like the Villa Comunale Park. Bring a camera to capture the beauty of the Amalfi Coast and Mount Vesuvius. Binoculars can also enhance your experience, allowing you to appreciate the details of the landscapes and architecture from a distance.

6. Italian Phrasebook:
While many locals in Sorrento speak English, having a basic understanding of Italian phrases can enhance your interactions and show appreciation for the local culture. Pack a small Italian phrasebook to help you navigate menus, ask for directions, and engage with the friendly locals.

7. Sunscreen and Toiletries:
Protect your skin from the Mediterranean sun by packing a high SPF sunscreen. Additionally, bring essential toiletries to ensure you stay fresh and comfortable throughout your trip.

8. Daypack:
A small daypack is handy for carrying essentials like water, snacks, a map, and your camera while exploring Sorrento. It's also useful for day trips to nearby attractions like Pompeii or the island of Capri.

9. Travel Guidebook:
While Sorrento is relatively small, a travel guidebook can provide valuable insights into the town's history, culture, and hidden gems. It can also help you plan day trips and discover local eateries.

10. Appetite for Culinary Delights:
Sorrento is renowned for its delicious cuisine, particularly its fresh seafood, limoncello, and mouthwatering pastries. Pack

an open mind and a hearty appetite to savor the local flavors and culinary delights that Sorrento has to offer.

By packing thoughtfully for your visit to Sorrento, you'll be well-prepared to soak in the beauty of this enchanting Italian town and create lasting memories of your Mediterranean getaway. Buon viaggio!

Trip Planning Tools

To make the most of your trip, it's essential to have the right planning tools at your fingertips. From navigating the narrow streets to finding the best local gems, here's a comprehensive guide to trip planning tools for your visit to Sorrento.

First and foremost, a reliable map app is a must. Sorrento's winding streets and alleys can be charming but also a bit confusing. Google Maps or Maps.me can be your best friends here, providing real-time navigation and helping you explore the town with ease. Download the offline maps in advance to ensure you won't get lost, especially if you plan on venturing into the Amalfi Coast or exploring nearby towns.

Language can sometimes be a barrier, but worry not! Language translation apps like Google Translate can assist you in bridging communication gaps. The locals always appreciate a visitor who makes an effort to speak their language, so having a few basic Italian phrases on hand can go a long way. Pair this with a good phrasebook app, and you'll find yourself connecting with the locals in no time.

To soak in the beauty of Sorrento's coastline and neighboring islands, consider using ferry schedule apps like Ferryhopper. This tool provides up-to-date information on ferry routes, schedules, and ticket prices, making it easy for you to plan a day trip to Capri or explore the Amalfi Coast at your own pace. Be sure to check the schedules in advance, especially during peak tourist seasons.

When it comes to accommodations, platforms like Airbnb, Booking.com, and TripAdvisor can help you find the perfect place to stay. Whether you prefer a charming boutique hotel with a sea view or a cozy Airbnb in the heart of the town, these platforms offer a wide range of options to suit every traveler's preferences and budget.

For food enthusiasts, apps like Yelp or TripAdvisor are indispensable. Sorrento is known for its delectable seafood, traditional Italian pizzas, and refreshing limoncello. Use these apps to discover hidden culinary gems, read reviews, and ensure you savor the best of Sorrento's gastronomic delights.

When planning your itinerary, consider using travel planning apps like TripIt or Sygic Travel. These tools allow you to organize your activities, reservations, and important information in one place, making your trip seamless and stress-free. Input your flight details, hotel reservations, and desired attractions, and let the app create a well-organized itinerary for you.

Don't forget to check the weather forecast using apps like AccuWeather or The Weather Channel. Sorrento's climate can vary, and knowing the weather conditions in advance will help you pack accordingly and plan your activities wisely.

To capture the essence of Sorrento, consider using photography apps like Instagram or VSCO. The town is a visual feast, with its colorful buildings, vibrant markets, and stunning seascapes. These apps can enhance your photos and help you share your travel adventures with friends and followers. Don't forget to use relevant hashtags to connect with other travelers and discover additional tips and recommendations.

For those interested in history and culture, museum guide apps like GuidiGO or Rick Steves Audio Europe can provide insightful information about Sorrento's historical sites and landmarks. Whether you're exploring the Cathedral of Sorrento, the Sedile Dominova, or the Chiesa di San Francesco, these apps offer audio guides and interactive maps to enrich your cultural experience.

If you're an avid hiker or nature enthusiast, trail mapping apps like AllTrails can guide you through the scenic trails surrounding Sorrento. Explore the renowned Path of the Gods on the Amalfi Coast or embark on a hike through the Lattari Mountains for panoramic views of the Mediterranean. These apps offer detailed trail maps, difficulty ratings, and user reviews to ensure you find the perfect route for your adventure.

Staying connected is crucial, and having a reliable Wi-Fi finder app like WiFi Map can be a lifesaver. Whether you need to quickly upload a stunning sunset photo or navigate the streets using an online map, these apps help you locate Wi-Fi hotspots in Sorrento and stay connected throughout your journey.

To manage your expenses and currency conversion, financial apps like XE Currency or Trail Wallet can be invaluable. Keep track of your spending, convert currencies on the go, and stay within your budget while enjoying all that Sorrento has to offer.

If you're a fan of spontaneous exploration, consider using geocaching apps to uncover hidden treasures and surprises scattered around Sorrento. Geocaching adds an element of adventure to your trip, leading you to unique locations and providing a different perspective on the town.

Lastly, keep abreast of local events and festivals with event discovery apps like Eventbrite or Meetup. Sorrento hosts various cultural events, concerts, and festivals throughout the year. Attending these events allows you to immerse yourself in the local culture and create lasting memories.

Armed with these trip planning tools, your visit to Sorrento is sure to be a memorable and smooth experience. Embrace the beauty of the Amalfi Coast, indulge in the local flavors, and let the charm of Sorrento captivate your heart. Buon viaggio!

Best Neighborhood to stay

When it comes to choosing the best neighborhood to stay in Sorrento, there are several factors to consider, including proximity to attractions, local ambiance, and accessibility. Let's explore some of the top neighborhoods that offer a delightful experience for visitors.

One of the most popular neighborhoods in Sorrento is the historic town center, often referred to as the Centro Storico. This area is a picturesque maze of narrow streets, lined with colorful buildings, local shops, and inviting cafes. Staying in the Centro Storico provides easy access to some of Sorrento's iconic landmarks, such as Piazza Tasso, the central square surrounded by restaurants and bars, and the 15th-century Sedil Dominova, a historic building with a distinctive octagonal shape. Choosing accommodation in this area allows you to immerse yourself in the rich history and vibrant atmosphere of Sorrento.

For those seeking a more relaxed and scenic environment, the Marina Grande neighborhood is an excellent choice. This charming fishing village is located below the town center, offering a tranquil escape from the bustling streets above. The Marina Grande beach is a hidden gem, with colorful boats bobbing in the crystal-clear waters. It's a perfect spot to unwind, enjoy fresh seafood at local restaurants, and take in breathtaking views of the coastline. While the Marina Grande area is quieter than the town center, it's just a short walk or bus ride away from the main attractions.

If you prefer a mix of tranquility and proximity to Sorrento's cultural highlights, the Sant'Agnello neighborhood is worth considering. Located just a short distance from the town center, Sant'Agnello offers a more laid-back atmosphere with beautiful gardens and scenic walks. This area is home to the Fondazione Sorrento, a cultural center housed in a historic villa that hosts art exhibitions, concerts, and other events. Choosing accommodation in Sant'Agnello provides a peaceful retreat while keeping you well-connected to Sorrento's main attractions.

For those who appreciate a touch of luxury and exclusivity, the Piano di Sorrento neighborhood is an upscale option. This area is known for its elegant villas, upscale hotels, and manicured gardens. It provides a quieter setting while still being within reach of Sorrento's center. The Villa Fondi, a beautiful estate with stunning views of the Gulf of Naples, is a notable attraction in Piano di Sorrento. Staying in this neighborhood allows you to experience Sorrento with a touch of sophistication and enjoy the serenity of the surrounding landscapes.

Sorrento offers a diverse range of neighborhoods, each with its unique charm and appeal. Whether you prefer the historic ambiance of the Centro Storico, the seaside tranquility of

Marina Grande, the cultural richness of Sant'Agnello, or the upscale atmosphere of Piano di Sorrento, there's a neighborhood that suits every traveler's preferences. Consider your priorities, whether they be proximity to attractions, a peaceful retreat, or a touch of luxury, and choose the neighborhood that aligns with your Sorrento dream getaway.

Accommodation

When planning a visit to Sorrento, one of the most picturesque and charming destinations on the Amalfi Coast, finding the perfect accommodation is key to ensuring a memorable and enjoyable stay. Sorrento offers a wide range of accommodation options, from luxury hotels with stunning sea views to cozy bed and breakfasts nestled in the narrow streets of the historic center.

For those seeking a touch of luxury, Sorrento boasts several upscale hotels that provide not only lavish accommodations but also exceptional service. One such option is the Grand Hotel Excelsior Vittoria, a five-star hotel perched on the cliffs overlooking the Bay of Naples. With its classic Italian elegance, beautiful gardens, and panoramic views, this hotel offers a truly indulgent experience. Guests can unwind in spacious, tastefully decorated rooms, enjoy gourmet dining at the hotel's restaurants, and relax by the pool while taking in the breathtaking scenery.

If you prefer a more intimate and personalized experience, Sorrento's boutique hotels may be the perfect choice. The Maison La Minervetta is a charming boutique hotel with a unique personality. Situated on the cliffside, it provides stunning views of the Tyrrhenian Sea. Each room is individually decorated with a mix of modern and vintage elements, creating a cozy and stylish atmosphere. The attentive staff adds a personal touch, making guests feel like they are staying in a home away from home.

For those on a more modest budget, Sorrento offers a variety of affordable accommodation options without compromising on comfort. Guesthouses and bed and breakfasts, such as the Palazzo Starace, provide a cozy and authentic experience. Located in the heart of the historic center, these establishments often feature charming rooms adorned with local artwork and offer a warm and welcoming atmosphere. The Palazzo Starace, for example, is housed in a historic building, providing guests with a taste of Sorrento's rich history.

If you prefer a self-catering option or a more independent stay, Sorrento has a range of vacation rentals and apartments available. These options allow visitors to experience the town like a local, with the flexibility to explore at their own pace. Whether it's a quaint apartment with a balcony overlooking the bustling streets or a villa nestled in the quiet hills surrounding Sorrento, these accommodations provide a homey and authentic experience.

When it comes to location, the choice of accommodation in Sorrento largely depends on your preferences and interests. Staying in the heart of the historic center allows easy access to Sorrento's vibrant streets, filled with charming shops, local markets, and traditional restaurants serving delicious Italian cuisine. On the other hand, choosing a hotel or villa along the coastline provides a tranquil retreat with mesmerizing sea views and the soothing sounds of the waves.

However, there are numerous apps available for finding and booking accommodations at your convenience, catering to various preferences and budgets. Here are some examples:

Booking.com: This app offers a wide range of accommodation options, including hotels, resorts, vacation rentals, and more. It provides user reviews and competitive pricing.

Airbnb: Airbnb is well-known for its vacation rental listings, offering unique stays such as apartments, homes, and even unconventional properties. It's perfect for travelers looking for a more local and immersive experience.

Expedia: Expedia is a comprehensive travel platform that allows you to book hotels, flights, and rental cars. It offers a loyalty program that can earn you rewards and discounts on future bookings.

Hostelworld: If you're seeking budget accommodations like hostels and budget hotels, Hostelworld is a top choice. It specializes in affordable and social accommodation options.

TripAdvisor: TripAdvisor provides a vast amount of user-generated content, including reviews, photos, and travel advice. It's an excellent resource for researching accommodations and finding user-recommended places to stay.

Hotels.com: Hotels.com is known for its straightforward interface and user-friendly rewards program. You can earn a free night's stay for every ten nights booked through the platform.

Agoda: Agoda is particularly popular in Asia and offers competitive rates on accommodations in the region. It's a great option for travelers exploring Asian destinations.

Vrbo (Vacation Rentals by Owner): Vrbo specializes in vacation home rentals, making it a top choice for travelers looking for spacious and private accommodations, including cottages, villas, and cabins.

Couchsurfing: Couchsurfing connects hosts willing to offer a free place to stay with guests. It's a unique way to meet locals and experience a destination from a different perspective.

Kayak: Kayak is a comprehensive travel app that compares prices on hotels, flights, and rental cars. It also offers a feature called "Price Alerts" to notify you when prices drop for your desired accommodations.

HotelTonight: HotelTonight specializes in last-minute hotel bookings, often at discounted rates. It's an excellent option for spontaneous travelers or those seeking a deal on short notice.

Instead of recommending hotels, guesthouses or resorts as the case maybe, we believe every traveler should have the freedom to use the apps to choose the accommodation of their choice because;

Every traveler is unique, and their travel preferences vary widely. Some may prefer the comfort and amenities of a hotel or resort, while others might seek a more immersive experience through vacation rentals or hostels. Allowing travelers to choose from a variety of apps ensures that they can find accommodation that suits their specific needs and desires.

Different travelers have different budgets for their trips. Some may be willing to splurge on luxury accommodations, while others may need to stick to a strict budget. These apps offer options at various price points, ensuring that travelers can find a place to stay that aligns with their financial capabilities.

Different Travelers have distinct travel styles. Some prefer a more structured and luxurious experience, while others seek adventure, social interactions, or an intimate, local feel. The array of apps provides options for solo travelers, families, couples, backpackers, business travelers, and everyone in between.

Apps like Airbnb and Vrbo enable tourists to experience a destination like a local by staying in private homes or unique, non-traditional properties. This offers a chance to immerse themselves in local culture, interact with residents, and explore neighborhoods that they might miss in traditional tourist areas.

These apps typically allow travelers to customize their search criteria. Travelers can specify the number of guests, location, amenities, and other factors to find accommodations that suit their specific requirements. This level of customization ensures that tourists have more control over their travel experience.

Competition among these apps can result in competitive pricing. This benefits travelers by driving down costs and offering a wide range of discounts and deals. Tourists can shop around to find the best deals and maximize the value of their travel budget.

Many of these booking apps provide user reviews and ratings for properties. This valuable feedback helps tourists make informed decisions about where to stay. It empowers them to avoid potential issues and choose accommodations that align with their expectations.

Regardless of the type of accommodation you choose, Sorrento's warm and welcoming atmosphere will make your stay truly special. The town's unique blend of history, culture, and natural beauty creates an enchanting backdrop for your visit. Whether you spend your days exploring ancient ruins, lounging on the beach, or savoring authentic Italian gelato in the town square, your choice of accommodation will enhance the overall experience of your Sorrento getaway.

Chapter 2: Top Tourist Attractions & Spots

Sorrento is a stunning coastal town in southern Italy, nestled in the picturesque region of Campania. With its breathtaking views, rich history, and vibrant culture, Sorrento is a top destination for travelers seeking a perfect blend of relaxation and exploration. In this extensive guide, we'll explore the top tourist attractions and spots that make Sorrento a must-visit destination.

1. Piazza Tasso:

Nestled in the heart of Sorrento, Piazza Tasso is a captivating square that encapsulates the very essence of this charming Italian town. Named after the celebrated poet Torquato Tasso, this lively square serves as a central meeting point, a cultural hub, and a gateway to the myriad wonders that Sorrento has to offer.

The square is easily accessible, located at the intersection of Via Santa Maria della Pieta and Corso Italia, making it a convenient starting point for exploring the town's treasures. The energetic atmosphere of Piazza Tasso is palpable from the moment you step onto its cobblestone streets. Its strategic location ensures that it is often the first glimpse visitors have of Sorrento's unique blend of history and modernity.

Surrounded by a harmonious blend of charming cafes, boutique shops, and historic buildings, Piazza Tasso offers a delightful mix of experiences. The cafes that line the square invite you to savor a leisurely cup of coffee or indulge in a delicious Italian gelato while immersing yourself in the lively ambiance. The outdoor seating allows you to soak in the surroundings and witness the ebb and flow of Sorrento's daily life.

As you explore the square, you'll encounter architectural gems that speak to the town's rich history. The Baroque Church of Saint Antonino, dedicated to Sorrento's patron saint, is a prominent feature of the square. Its intricate facade and artistic embellishments provide a glimpse into the town's religious heritage.

For those inclined towards shopping, the boutiques and shops that adorn Piazza Tasso offer a delightful array of local and artisanal products. From intricately crafted ceramics to handmade leather goods, the square is a treasure trove for those seeking unique souvenirs.

If you wish to delve deeper into Sorrento's history, take a stroll towards the Sorrento Foundation, located on Via Santa Maria della Pieta. This cultural institution hosts exhibitions and events that provide insights into the town's past and present. It's a hidden gem that adds an enriching layer to your exploration of Piazza Tasso.

As the sun sets, Piazza Tasso transforms into a magical space illuminated by the warm glow of streetlights and the vibrant energy of the surrounding establishments. The square becomes a focal point for evening strolls and social gatherings, making it a perfect place to unwind after a day of exploration.

Piazza Tasso is not merely a square; it is the beating heart of Sorrento. Its dynamic energy, historical significance, and convenient location make it an indispensable part of any Sorrento itinerary. So, when you find yourself in Sorrento, let Piazza Tasso be your starting point—a gateway to the town's enchanting tapestry of culture, history, and modern life.

2. Marina Grande:

Marina Grande, nestled on the Sorrento coastline, is a captivating destination that transports visitors to the authentic charm of an Italian fishing village. Located just a short stroll from the bustling Piazza Tasso, Marina Grande is a picturesque harbor that embodies the laid-back Mediterranean lifestyle.

As you make your way towards Marina Grande, the cobbled streets wind down to the waterfront, revealing a postcard-perfect scene of colorful buildings that hug the shoreline. These buildings, adorned with vibrant shutters and flower-filled balconies, create a captivating backdrop against the azure waters of the Tyrrhenian Sea. The atmosphere is both tranquil and inviting, making it a perfect escape from the lively energy of the town center.

Seafood enthusiasts will find Marina Grande to be a culinary haven. The waterfront is lined with charming seafood restaurants that beckon visitors with the enticing aroma of freshly caught fish and seafood delicacies. From traditional pasta dishes infused with the flavors of the sea to grilled specialties, Marina Grande's eateries showcase the region's culinary prowess. Savoring a meal on one of the open-air terraces, with the sound of lapping waves and the sea breeze in the air, is a sensory experience that captures the essence of Sorrento's coastal charm.

For those seeking a bit of history, the harbor is dotted with small, colorful boats that bob gently on the water. These traditional fishing vessels, with their weathered charm, add a touch of authenticity to the scene. Strolling along the water's edge, visitors can witness local fishermen tending to their nets and boats, providing a glimpse into the timeless maritime traditions that have shaped the character of Marina Grande.

To fully immerse yourself in the ambiance of Marina Grande, consider exploring the narrow alleyways that meander through the village. These alleys are adorned with vibrant bougainvillea, and each turn unveils hidden gems, from quaint cafes serving espresso to artisanal shops offering locally crafted souvenirs.

For those eager to visit Marina Grande, its address is easily accessible. Located at Via Marina Grande, 1, 80067 Sorrento NA, Italy, it is a convenient and enjoyable walk from the heart of Sorrento. The journey allows visitors to soak in the stunning coastal views and gradually transition from the lively town center to the tranquil haven of Marina Grande.

Marina Grande is a gem within Sorrento that beckons with its authentic fishing village charm. Whether you are savoring seafood delights, exploring historic alleyways, or simply basking in the serene ambiance, Marina Grande offers a delightful escape that lingers in the hearts of those who experience its enchanting allure.

3. Sorrento Cathedral:

Located in the heart of Sorrento, the Sorrento Cathedral stands as a testament to the town's rich religious and architectural heritage. Dedicated to Saints Philip and James, this medieval masterpiece is a must-visit for travelers seeking a profound connection to both history and spirituality.

The cathedral's address, Corso Italia, 248, 80067 Sorrento NA, Italy, places it conveniently in the town center, making it easily accessible for visitors exploring the charming streets of Sorrento.

Architectural Marvel:

Stepping through the cathedral's entrance, visitors are immediately enveloped in an aura of reverence and awe. The architecture, dating back to the 15th century, showcases a harmonious blend of Gothic, Baroque, and Renaissance styles. The facade is adorned with intricate detailing, including arches, columns, and sculptures that narrate stories of religious significance.

Interior Splendor:
Once inside, the cathedral's interior captivates with its grandeur. The nave, supported by Corinthian columns, leads the eyes towards the ornate altar. Frescoes depicting biblical scenes adorn the walls, each stroke of paint telling a story that echoes through centuries. The play of light filtering through stained glass windows adds an ethereal quality to the space.

Altar of Reverence:
The grand altar, the focal point of the cathedral, is a masterpiece of craftsmanship. Carved from marble, it depicts scenes from the life of Saints Philip and James, inviting worshippers and art enthusiasts alike to contemplate the divine narratives immortalized in stone.

Bell Tower Vista:
Adjacent to the cathedral is a soaring bell tower that beckons visitors to ascend its ancient steps. The climb is rewarded with breathtaking panoramic views of Sorrento and the Bay of Naples. The red-tiled roofs of the town contrast against the azure sea, creating a vista that lingers in the memory long after the descent.

Religious Significance:
Beyond its architectural and artistic magnificence, Sorrento Cathedral holds deep religious significance for the local community. It remains a place of worship and pilgrimage,

where both locals and visitors gather to seek solace, reflect, and partake in the timeless rituals of the Catholic faith.

Cultural Preservation:
Efforts to preserve the cathedral's cultural heritage are evident in ongoing restoration projects. These endeavors ensure that future generations can continue to marvel at the intricate details, study the artistry of bygone eras, and appreciate the spiritual ambiance that permeates the sacred space.

Visiting Sorrento Cathedral is not just a journey through time and architecture; it is a spiritual odyssey that connects visitors to the profound cultural and religious roots of the town. As you stand in awe of the cathedral's beauty, you become part of a tradition that spans centuries, embracing the sacred and the artistic in one harmonious experience.

4. Villa Comunale:

Nestled high on the cliffs overlooking the azure waters of the Gulf of Naples, Villa Comunale stands as a serene haven amidst the vibrant energy of Sorrento. Located at Via San Francesco, 1, this beautiful public garden is a testament to the town's commitment to preserving its natural beauty while providing a haven for locals and visitors alike.

As you make your way to Villa Comunale, the anticipation builds with each step, and upon arrival, you're greeted by a breathtaking panorama that stretches as far as the eye can see. The well-manicured gardens, adorned with a kaleidoscope of flora, create a vibrant tapestry against the backdrop of the sea. Bougainvillea bursts forth in a riot of colors, while fragrant roses perfume the air, enhancing the sensory experience of this enchanting oasis.

The meticulous landscaping of Villa Comunale is a testament to the town's dedication to preserving green spaces. Olive trees, iconic to the Mediterranean landscape, provide shade and a sense of timelessness, inviting visitors to linger and appreciate the simple pleasures of nature. Meandering pathways wind through the garden, leading you to hidden corners and secluded spots, perfect for quiet contemplation or an intimate conversation.

Statues and sculptures, strategically placed throughout the garden, add a touch of artistry to the natural surroundings. These elegant works of art pay homage to Sorrento's rich cultural heritage, providing a harmonious blend of nature and history. Each statue tells a story, inviting visitors to pause and reflect on the timeless beauty that surrounds them.

Villa Comunale is more than just a garden; it's a sensory experience that captures the essence of Sorrento. The sound of the waves crashing against the cliffs below, the scent of blooming flowers, and the sight of the sun-drenched landscape create a symphony of sensations that transport you to a state of tranquility.

This idyllic spot is not only a visual feast but also a perfect setting for leisurely activities. Whether you choose to embark on a leisurely stroll along the pathways, find a secluded bench to read a book, or spread out a picnic blanket for a delightful afternoon repast, Villa Comunale accommodates every pace and preference. Families, couples, and solo travelers can all find their own corner of paradise within the garden's embrace.

Villa Comunale beckons you to experience the beauty of Sorrento in a way that transcends the ordinary, offering a retreat that rejuvenates the spirit and leaves an indelible mark on your travel memories. As you explore the garden, take a moment to absorb the ambiance, appreciate the details, and let the magic of Villa Comunale become a cherished chapter in your Sorrento adventure.

5. Correale Museum of Terracotta:

Art and history enthusiasts visiting Sorrento should not miss the Correale Museum of Terracotta, a cultural gem that offers a deep dive into the rich artistic heritage of the region. This museum, located at Via Correale, 50, 80067 Sorrento NA, Italy, is a testament to the town's commitment to preserving and showcasing its historical and artistic treasures.

The Correale Museum is housed in a magnificent historic villa that dates back to the 18th century. Its architecture alone is worth the visit, with the villa providing an elegant backdrop to the impressive collection within. The museum is conveniently located in the heart of Sorrento, making it easily accessible for tourists exploring the town center.

Upon entering the museum, visitors are greeted by a curated display of terracotta artifacts, a medium that has played a significant role in Italian art for centuries. From intricately crafted pottery to delicate sculptures, the collection spans various styles and periods, offering a comprehensive overview of the evolution of terracotta art in the region.

One of the highlights of the Correale Museum is its extensive collection of paintings, showcasing the works of renowned Italian artists. From Renaissance masterpieces to Baroque wonders, the museum's art collection provides a visual journey through the different artistic movements that have left their mark on Sorrento.

In addition to terracotta and paintings, the museum boasts a diverse array of decorative arts. Visitors can marvel at exquisite ceramics, ornate furniture, and other artifacts that reflect the craftsmanship and aesthetic sensibilities of the region over the centuries.

What sets the Correale Museum apart is its commitment to contextualizing the exhibited pieces within the broader historical and cultural narrative of Sorrento. Informative plaques and guided tours provide valuable insights into the significance of each artifact, enriching the visitor's experience and fostering a deeper appreciation for the artistic legacy of the town.

The museum's location within a historic villa adds another layer of charm to the overall experience. Surrounded by lush gardens, the villa provides a tranquil setting for visitors to wander and reflect. The well-maintained grounds offer a serene escape from the bustling streets of Sorrento, creating a harmonious balance between art, history, and nature.

Visitors can take advantage of guided tours to gain a more in-depth understanding of the museum's collection and history. Knowledgeable guides provide fascinating anecdotes and stories that breathe life into the artifacts, making the visit not just educational but also engaging and immersive.

Before leaving the Correale Museum, be sure to explore its gift shop, where you can find unique souvenirs inspired by the exhibited art. From terracotta replicas to art prints, the shop offers a chance to take a piece of Sorrento's artistic heritage home with you.

In conclusion, the Correale Museum of Terracotta is a must-visit destination for those seeking a cultural and artistic immersion in Sorrento. Its impressive collection, coupled with the charm of its historic villa and gardens, ensures a memorable experience that captures the essence of the town's rich heritage.

6. Sedile Dominova:

For a journey back in time to the heart of Sorrento's cultural and social life, a visit to Sedile Dominova is a must. This historic building, located at Largo Arcivescovado, 1, 80067 Sorrento NA, Italy, stands as a testament to the town's noble past and serves as a captivating stop for those interested in its cultural heritage.

Sedile Dominova, constructed in the 15th century, holds a prominent place in Sorrento's historic center. The building served as a meeting place for the local nobility, offering a venue for important discussions and social gatherings. Its name, "Sedile," refers to a seat or meeting place, and "Dominova" is a nod to the noble families who dominated the social scene in the town.

The architecture of Sedile Dominova is a prime example of Renaissance style, with its intricate detailing and harmonious proportions. The façade features elegant arches and columns, reflecting the influence of the Renaissance period and the aesthetic preferences of the local aristocracy.

Upon entering Sedile Dominova, visitors are transported to a bygone era. The interior is adorned with frescoes and decorations that speak to the opulence and sophistication of Sorrento's noble class. The grandeur of the building serves as a visual representation of the town's historical significance and its role as a hub for cultural and social exchange.

One of the notable features of Sedile Dominova is the large central hall, where meetings and gatherings took place. The architecture of this hall, with its vaulted ceilings and decorative elements, showcases the wealth and artistic sensibilities of Sorrento's elite during the Renaissance.

In addition to its architectural and historical significance, Sedile Dominova often hosts cultural events and exhibitions. These events provide a contemporary context for the building, ensuring that it remains a dynamic and relevant part of Sorrento's cultural landscape.

To enhance the visitor experience, Sedile Dominova offers guided tours that provide insights into the history of the building and its role in shaping the town's cultural identity. Knowledgeable guides share stories and anecdotes, offering a deeper understanding of the social dynamics and historical events that unfolded within the walls of Sedile Dominova.

As you explore the building, take a moment to appreciate the panoramic views of Sorrento's historic center from its vantage point. The location of Sedile Dominova allows for a unique perspective of the town, providing a visual connection between its noble past and the vibrant present.

Before leaving, consider exploring the surrounding area, as Sedile Dominova is nestled in the heart of Sorrento's bustling streets. Cafes, shops, and other historic landmarks are within walking distance, allowing you to continue your journey through the town's captivating streetscape.

Sedile Dominova stands as a living testament to Sorrento's rich cultural heritage. Its historical significance, coupled with its stunning architecture, makes it a captivating destination for those eager to delve into the town's noble past and immerse themselves in its unique charm.

7. Vallone dei Mulini: A Journey Through Sorrento's Industrial Past

Address: Vallone dei Mulini, Via Fuorimura, 80067 Sorrento NA, Italy

Nestled amid the lush landscapes of Sorrento, Vallone dei Mulini, or the Valley of the Mills, stands as a testament to the town's industrial history. Located at Via Fuorimura, 80067 Sorrento NA, Italy, this deep ravine was once a hub of activity, home to several medieval mills that played a crucial role in Sorrento's economy.

History and Industrial Heritage:
The Vallone dei Mulini dates back to the 10th century, and its mills were primarily used for grinding wheat, a vital aspect of Sorrento's agricultural and economic activities during that time. The ravine's strategic location, with its abundant water supply from the natural springs, made it an ideal site for milling operations.

As you explore Vallone dei Mulini, you'll encounter the remnants of these medieval mills, their weathered stone walls standing as silent witnesses to centuries of industry. The well-preserved structures offer a fascinating glimpse into the ingenuity of the medieval craftsmen who built and operated these mills.

Scenic Hiking Opportunity:
Today, Vallone dei Mulini is a haven for nature lovers and hiking enthusiasts. The verdant surroundings, with dense

vegetation and towering trees, create a serene atmosphere as you traverse the hiking trails. The trails wind through the ravine, providing glimpses of the ancient mills and offering a unique blend of natural beauty and historical intrigue.

The hike through Vallone dei Mulini allows you to immerse yourself in the peaceful ambiance of the Sorrentine landscape while uncovering the layers of history hidden within its depths. As you ascend the trails, you'll be treated to panoramic views of Sorrento and the Bay of Naples, making the journey both enriching and visually stunning.

Address:
Vallone dei Mulini is easily accessible from the town center of Sorrento. The official address is Via Fuorimura, 80067 Sorrento NA, Italy. The entrance to the ravine is well-marked, and you can embark on your exploration directly from the heart of Sorrento.

Tips for Visitors:

- Wear Comfortable Footwear: The hiking trails in Vallone dei Mulini can be uneven, so it's advisable to wear comfortable and sturdy footwear suitable for walking.
- Bring Water and Snacks: Ensure you stay hydrated during your hike by bringing a water bottle. Consider packing some snacks to enjoy amidst the picturesque surroundings.
- Explore at Your Own Pace: Take your time exploring the ravine and its mills. The beauty of Vallone dei Mulini lies not just in its history but in the tranquility it offers, so feel free to set your own pace.

8. Church of St. Francis: A Sanctuary of Art and Tranquility

Address: Church of St. Francis, Piazza Sant'Antonino, 3, 80067 Sorrento NA, Italy

Tucked away in a quiet corner of Sorrento, the Church of St. Francis is a hidden gem that beckons visitors with its simple yet elegant architecture and a treasury of artistic treasures. Located at Piazza Sant'Antonino, 3, 80067 Sorrento NA, Italy, this church is a haven of peace and a refuge for those seeking a moment of quiet contemplation amidst the vibrant energy of Sorrento.

Architectural Beauty:
The Church of St. Francis, dating back to the 14th century, is a fine example of medieval architecture. Its unassuming exterior gives way to a serene interior adorned with arches, frescoes, and a sense of timeless tranquility. The architecture reflects the Franciscan ideals of simplicity and humility, creating a space that invites introspection and spiritual reflection.

Artistic Treasures:
Within the walls of the Church of St. Francis, art enthusiasts will discover a remarkable collection of paintings and sculptures spanning various periods. The works of art housed in the church provide a visual narrative of Sorrento's cultural and religious history, making it a valuable repository of artistic heritage.

One of the highlights of the church is the altar, a focal point adorned with intricate carvings and religious iconography.

The soft glow of natural light filtering through the windows enhances the ambiance, creating a contemplative atmosphere that adds to the overall experience.

Address:
The Church of St. Francis is centrally located in Sorrento, making it easily accessible for visitors. The official address is Piazza Sant'Antonino, 3, 80067 Sorrento NA, Italy. The church is situated in close proximity to other attractions in the historic center, allowing you to include it seamlessly in your exploration of Sorrento.

Tips for Visitors:

- Respectful Attire: As with many religious sites, it's advisable to dress modestly when visiting the Church of St. Francis out of respect for its sacred nature.
- Quiet Contemplation: Take a moment to sit quietly and absorb the peaceful atmosphere. The church's tranquil setting makes it an ideal place for reflection.
- Check for Events: The Church of St. Francis occasionally hosts cultural and religious events. Check the local calendar to see if any special events coincide with your visit.

9. Baths of Queen Giovanna: Unveiling Ancient Luxury

The Baths of Queen Giovanna, situated on the picturesque Sorrentine Peninsula, offer a captivating journey back in time to the opulent days of ancient Rome. Believed to be the remains of a seaside villa that once belonged to a Roman noblewoman, Queen Giovanna, these well-preserved ruins provide a fascinating glimpse into the lifestyle of the Roman elite.

Address: Via Capo, 80067 Sorrento NA, Italy

As you make your way to the Baths of Queen Giovanna, you'll be greeted by the gentle sea breeze and the sound of waves crashing against the nearby cliffs. The site is perched on the coast, surrounded by lush greenery, creating a serene and atmospheric setting that transports visitors to a bygone era.

The ruins showcase the architectural sophistication of the Romans, with remnants of rooms, corridors, and bathing areas. The strategic placement of the villa allows for breathtaking views of the Gulf of Naples, highlighting the Romans' appreciation for both luxury and natural beauty.

Wandering through the site, you'll encounter the remains of the baths, believed to have been fed by both seawater and freshwater springs. The engineering marvels of the ancient Romans become evident as you explore the intricate plumbing systems and well-preserved mosaic floors that once adorned this seaside retreat.

One notable feature is the natural cave known as the Grotta del Bagni della Regina Giovanna, which served as a private swimming area for the noble residents. The cave, with its crystal-clear waters, adds an air of mystique to the overall ambiance of the Baths. It's not hard to imagine Queen Giovanna herself enjoying moments of leisure in this secluded coastal haven.

Visitors are encouraged to take their time exploring the site, imagining the vibrant social gatherings, decadent banquets, and luxurious rituals that once took place within these ancient walls. The Baths of Queen Giovanna offer a unique perspective on the intersection of Roman opulence and the natural beauty of the Sorrentine coastline.

10. Sorrento Musical: A Symphony of Neapolitan Culture

Immerse yourself in the soul-stirring melodies and rhythmic dances of Sorrento by attending a performance at Sorrento Musical. This intimate venue, nestled in the heart of the town, is a cultural gem that celebrates the rich musical heritage of the region, particularly the traditional sounds of Neapolitan music.

Address: Corso Italia, 344, 80067 Sorrento NA, Italy

Sorrento Musical is more than just a performance; it's a journey into the heart of Neapolitan culture. The venue itself is an embodiment of Old World charm, with its warm ambiance, intimate seating, and a stage that has witnessed countless performances by local artists.

The musical performances at Sorrento Musical showcase a diverse range of traditional Neapolitan music, including classic songs, folk tunes, and dances that have been passed down through generations. The talented musicians and performers bring these age-old melodies to life, creating an authentic and immersive experience for the audience.

The evening begins with the enchanting sounds of mandolins, accordions, and guitars, setting the stage for a celebration of the vibrant musical traditions that define Sorrento and its surrounding regions. As the musicians play, skilled dancers take to the stage, their movements reflecting the passion and history embedded in each note.

One highlight of Sorrento Musical is the inclusion of tarantella, a lively and rhythmic folk dance that originated in Southern Italy. The infectious energy of the tarantella is sure to have you tapping your feet and, perhaps, joining in the revelry. The performers' colorful costumes and the lively atmosphere create a spectacle that captivates both the seasoned traveler and first-time visitor alike.

During intermissions, patrons have the opportunity to savor local delicacies and wines, further enhancing the overall experience. The fusion of music, dance, and culinary delights makes Sorrento Musical a comprehensive celebration of Neapolitan culture.

Whether you're a music enthusiast, a lover of dance, or someone eager to delve into the authentic spirit of Sorrento, Sorrento Musical promises an unforgettable evening filled with cultural richness and artistic expression. It's not merely a performance; it's a symphony of Neapolitan culture that resonates with the timeless essence of this enchanting coastal town.

11. Cooking Classes:

Sorrento's culinary scene is as vibrant as its coastal views, and there's no better way to immerse yourself in it than by taking a cooking class. Unleash your inner chef and learn the secrets of authentic Italian cuisine, guided by local experts who are passionate about preserving and sharing their culinary heritage.

Culinary Institute of Sorrento:
One of the most reputable institutions offering cooking classes is the Culinary Institute of Sorrento, located at Via Santa Maria della Pieta, 5. This institute prides itself on providing an immersive experience that goes beyond just

preparing recipes. Here, you'll delve into the history of Sorrentine cuisine, explore the significance of locally sourced ingredients, and master the art of creating traditional dishes.

The institute's classes cover a range of topics, from handmade pasta and pizza to the delicate art of dessert making. Expect a hands-on experience that takes you from selecting the freshest produce at local markets to crafting a multi-course meal. The classes are designed for all skill levels, ensuring both beginners and seasoned cooks can enjoy and learn.

Address:
Culinary Institute of Sorrento
Via Santa Maria della Pieta, 5
80067 Sorrento NA, Italy

La Cucina del Gusto:
For those looking for a more intimate setting, La Cucina del Gusto offers personalized cooking classes in a charming setting overlooking the Bay of Naples. Located at Via Fuorimura, 25, this culinary haven is dedicated to preserving Sorrento's culinary traditions while adding a modern touch.

Classes at La Cucina del Gusto cover a range of topics, including antipasti, fresh pasta, and regional specialties. The instructors, often local chefs with years of experience, guide participants through each step, providing insights into the cultural significance of each dish. The small class sizes allow for personalized attention, making it an ideal choice for those who want a tailored and in-depth cooking experience.

Address:
La Cucina del Gusto
Via Fuorimura, 25
80067 Sorrento NA, Italy

Cooking Vacations Italy:
For a more comprehensive experience, Cooking Vacations Italy, located at Via Casarlano, 38, offers not only cooking classes but also culinary vacations that combine hands-on cooking with local tours and tastings. This is an excellent option for travelers seeking an immersive journey into Sorrento's gastronomic delights.

Cooking Vacations Italy collaborates with local chefs and farmers to provide a holistic experience. Classes often start with a visit to Sorrento's vibrant markets to select fresh ingredients, followed by hands-on cooking in a picturesque kitchen setting. The experience extends beyond the class, with participants having the opportunity to explore the region's wineries, olive groves, and historical sites.

Address:
Cooking Vacations Italy
Via Casarlano, 38
80067 Sorrento NA, Italy

12. Lemon Groves:

Sorrento's claim to fame is undoubtedly its luscious lemons, and a visit to one of the local lemon groves is a sensory journey that should not be missed. The fragrant aroma of citrus in the air, coupled with the picturesque landscape, creates an unforgettable experience.

Limonoro:
Limonoro, situated at Via Correale, 25, is a family-owned lemon grove that opens its doors to visitors eager to learn about the cultivation of Sorrento's prized lemons. The guided tours take you through the groves, explaining the meticulous

care that goes into growing these unique lemons and the importance of their role in local cuisine.

The visit to Limonoro often includes a tasting session where you can sample freshly squeezed lemon juice, limoncello, and lemon-infused olive oil. The owners share their family's history of lemon farming, offering a personal touch that enhances the overall experience.

Address:
Limonoro
Via Correale, 25
80067 Sorrento NA, Italy

Gargiulo & Jannuzzi:
Another notable lemon grove to explore is Gargiulo & Jannuzzi, located at Via Padre Reginaldo Giuliani, 57. This family-run farm not only showcases the art of lemon cultivation but also provides insights into the production of limoncello and other lemon-based products.

The guided tours at Gargiulo & Jannuzzi offer a behind-the-scenes look at the various stages of lemon cultivation, from planting to harvesting. Visitors can also witness the traditional method of making limoncello and taste the final product. The farm's idyllic setting makes it a perfect spot for capturing memorable photos of Sorrento's iconic lemon groves.

Address:
Gargiulo & Jannuzzi
Via Padre Reginaldo Giuliani, 57
80067 Sorrento NA, Italy

Agruminato:
Agruminato, nestled at Via Casarlano, 2, is a lemon and citrus farm that combines tradition with innovation. This

eco-friendly grove focuses on organic cultivation practices, providing a unique perspective on sustainable agriculture in the region.

Guided tours at Agruminato include a walk through the groves, where visitors can learn about organic farming techniques and the importance of biodiversity in maintaining the health of the lemon trees. The farm also offers interactive workshops on making lemon-infused products, allowing participants to create their own souvenirs to take home.

Address:
Agruminato
Via Casarlano, 2
80067 Sorrento NA, Italy

Exploring Sorrento's lemon groves not only offers a delightful olfactory experience but also provides a deeper understanding of the cultural and economic significance of lemons in this coastal paradise. From cooking classes to strolls through fragrant groves, these experiences are a feast for the senses, allowing visitors to savor the essence of Sorrento long after their journey concludes.

13. Capri Day Trip: Exploring the Jewel of the Mediterranean

A visit to Sorrento wouldn't be complete without a day trip to the enchanting island of Capri. Just a short ferry ride from Sorrento's Marina Piccola, Capri is a jewel in the Mediterranean, known for its stunning landscapes, glamorous atmosphere, and natural wonders. Here's a detailed guide to make the most of your Capri day trip:

How to Get There:
Start your journey by taking a ferry from Sorrento's Marina Piccola to Capri. The ferry ride itself is a delightful experience, offering panoramic views of the Gulf of Naples and the rugged coastline. The journey takes approximately 20-30 minutes, and the regular ferry services make it convenient for day-trippers.

Blue Grotto:
One of the must-see attractions on Capri is the Blue Grotto (Grotta Azzurra), a mesmerizing sea cave illuminated by an ethereal blue light. To reach the cave, you can take a small boat from Marina Grande, Capri's main port. The entrance to the cave is tiny, so you'll need to lie back in the boat as you enter. Once inside, the magical play of light on the water creates a surreal and unforgettable experience.

Address for Blue Grotto Boat Tours:
Marina Grande, 80073 Capri NA, Italy

Capri Town and Piazzetta:
After exploring the Blue Grotto, head to Capri Town, the island's main hub. The Piazzetta, or little square, is the heart of Capri, surrounded by cafes, boutiques, and charming architecture. Take a leisurely stroll, enjoy a coffee in one of the bustling cafes, and soak in the glamorous atmosphere. The Piazzetta is a perfect spot for people-watching and immersing yourself in the island's chic lifestyle.

Address for Piazzetta:
Piazza Umberto I, 80076 Capri NA, Italy

Gardens of Augustus:
For panoramic views of the Faraglioni rock formations and the sea, visit the Gardens of Augustus (Giardini di Augusto). These beautifully landscaped gardens are adorned with

colorful flowers and offer a tranquil escape from the bustling streets. The vantage points within the gardens provide stunning photo opportunities of Capri's iconic natural beauty.

Address for Gardens of Augustus:
Viale Matteotti, 2, 80076 Capri NA, Italy

Anacapri and Villa San Michele:
Take a bus or a scenic chairlift to Anacapri, the quieter and less crowded part of the island. Explore the charming streets, visit the historic Church of San Michele, and make your way to Villa San Michele. This villa, once the home of Swedish physician and author Axel Munthe, is now a museum with beautiful gardens and breathtaking views of the Gulf of Naples.

Address for Villa San Michele:
Viale Axel Munthe, 34, 80071 Anacapri NA, Italy

Lunch at a Seaside Restaurant:
Capri offers a variety of exquisite dining options, from upscale restaurants to quaint seaside cafes. Indulge in fresh seafood, traditional Italian dishes, and the island's renowned limoncello. Choose a restaurant with a view of the sea to enhance your dining experience.

Marina Piccola:
Before heading back to Sorrento, take a moment to visit Marina Piccola, Capri's smaller but equally charming port. Enjoy the serene atmosphere, take in the views of the crystalline waters, and perhaps dip your toes in the inviting Mediterranean Sea.

Address for Marina Piccola:
Marina Piccola, 80076 Capri NA, Italy

14. Amalfi Coast Drive: A Scenic Journey Along the Coastal Marvel

The Amalfi Coast, a UNESCO World Heritage site, is renowned for its dramatic cliffs, picturesque villages, and breathtaking views of the Tyrrhenian Sea. Embark on a scenic drive along the Amalfi Coast, a journey that promises to be one of the most memorable road trips of your life.

Starting Point: Sorrento to Positano:
Begin your Amalfi Coast adventure by driving from Sorrento to Positano. The winding coastal roads offer jaw-dropping views at every turn. As you approach Positano, you'll be greeted by pastel-colored buildings cascading down the cliffs, creating a postcard-perfect scene.

Address for Positano:
Via Cristoforo Colombo, 30, 84017 Positano SA, Italy

Exploring Positano:
Park your car and explore the narrow streets of Positano on foot. Visit the Church of Santa Maria Assunta, relax on the beaches, and indulge in shopping for handmade ceramics and local crafts. Positano's charm lies in its laid-back atmosphere and the stunning contrast between the colorful buildings and the azure sea.

Amalfi:
Continue your journey towards Amalfi, stopping at picturesque viewpoints along the way. Amalfi, with its historic cathedral and vibrant town center, is a gem nestled between the cliffs and the sea. Visit the Cathedral of Saint

Andrew (Cattedrale di Sant'Andrea) and stroll through the lively Piazza del Duomo.

Address for Cathedral of Saint Andrew:
Piazza Duomo, 84011 Amalfi SA, Italy

Ravello:
A short drive from Amalfi, Ravello is perched high above the coast, offering panoramic views and a more tranquil setting. Explore the gardens of Villa Cimbrone and Villa Rufolo, both of which provide stunning vistas of the coastline. Ravello's serene ambiance and cultural richness make it a hidden gem of the Amalfi Coast.

Address for Villa Cimbrone:
Via Santa Chiara, 26, 84010 Ravello SA, Italy

Address for Villa Rufolo:
Piazza Duomo, 84010 Ravello SA, Italy

Atrani and Minori:
As you drive back towards Sorrento, make a stop in the charming villages of Atrani and Minori. These less touristy spots offer a more authentic experience of local life on the Amalfi Coast. Wander through the narrow streets, visit local cafes, and enjoy the laid-back ambiance.

Address for Atrani:
Piazza Umberto I, 84010 Atrani SA, Italy

Address for Minori:
Via Roma, 82, 84010 Minori SA, Italy

Sunset in Sorrento:
Conclude your Amalfi Coast drive by returning to Sorrento in time to witness a spectacular sunset. Whether you choose to

view it from the cliffs of Villa Comunale or the bustling Piazza Tasso, the sunset over the Gulf of Naples is a fitting end to your day of exploration.

Address for Villa Comunale:
Via San Francesco, 1, 80067 Sorrento NA, Italy

15. Hiking the Path of the Gods:

The Path of the Gods, or Sentiero degli Dei, is a must-visit for outdoor enthusiasts seeking a memorable hiking experience in the stunning Amalfi Coast. This ancient trail winds its way through lush landscapes, offering hikers breathtaking views of the Mediterranean, ancient ruins, and dramatic cliffs.

Starting in the town of Bomerano, the trail extends towards Nocelle, providing a challenging yet rewarding trek that takes approximately 4 to 5 hours to complete. The path is well-marked, making it accessible for hikers of varying skill levels. Along the way, you'll encounter the remnants of old farmhouses, vineyards, and terraced fields, showcasing the region's rich agricultural history.

One of the highlights of the hike is the spectacular view of Positano from above. As you ascend, the panorama unfolds, revealing the colorful buildings perched on the cliffs and the azure sea stretching out endlessly. The sense of accomplishment upon reaching the highest point of the trail is unparalleled, offering a feeling of being on top of the world.

The Path of the Gods is not just a physical journey; it's a sensory experience. The scent of wildflowers, the chirping of birds, and the gentle breeze from the sea create an immersive connection with nature. Be sure to bring a camera

to capture the awe-inspiring landscapes and memorable moments along the way.
Address:
Sentiero degli Dei, 80051 Agerola NA, Italy

Tips for Hiking the Path of the Gods:

- Wear comfortable hiking shoes: The trail can be uneven, so proper footwear is essential for a safe and enjoyable hike.
- Bring sufficient water: Staying hydrated is crucial, especially on a sunny day. Carry an adequate supply of water to keep you energized throughout the hike.
- Pack a picnic: There are ideal spots along the trail to stop and enjoy a picnic with panoramic views. Pack some local cheeses, olives, and fresh fruit for a delightful break.
- Check the weather: While the trail is open year-round, it's advisable to check the weather forecast before embarking on the hike. Clear skies enhance the beauty of the surroundings.
- Start early: Begin your hike early in the day to avoid the heat and crowds. The morning light also adds a magical quality to the landscape.

16. Wine Tasting in the Hills:

Sorrento's surrounding hills are not only a feast for the eyes but also home to vineyards producing some of the finest local wines. A wine-tasting tour in this picturesque setting is a delightful way to immerse yourself in the flavors of Sorrento's terroir.

Cantine Marisa Cuomo:

Nestled on the cliffs of Furore, Cantine Marisa Cuomo is a renowned winery that combines tradition with innovation. The vineyards are perched on steep slopes overlooking the sea, creating a unique microclimate that influences the character of the grapes. Take a guided tour to explore the vineyards, cellars, and learn about the winemaking process. The tasting sessions here often include a selection of their signature wines, such as the famous Furore Bianco Fiorduva and the intense Amalfi Costa d'Amalfi Rosso.

Address:
Cantine Marisa Cuomo, Via G.B. Lama, 16, 84010 Furore SA, Italy

Villa Dora - Sorrentino Winery:
Located in the hills above Sorrento, Villa Dora is a family-run winery that has been producing wine for generations. The vineyards benefit from the volcanic soil and the Mediterranean climate, imparting a unique character to the wines. A visit to Villa Dora includes a guided tour of the vineyards and cellars, followed by a tasting of their diverse range of wines, including the crisp Falanghina and the robust Tintore.

Address:
Villa Dora - Sorrentino Winery, Via San Michele, 10, 80067 Sorrento NA, Italy

Azienda Agricola Forestaro:
For a more intimate and rustic wine-tasting experience, head to Azienda Agricola Forestaro. This small, family-owned winery is tucked away in the hills near Sant'Agata sui Due Golfi. The passionate winemakers here offer personalized tours, sharing insights into their winemaking philosophy and the unique characteristics of the local grape varieties. The

tasting sessions often include a selection of their organic wines, providing a genuine and authentic experience.

Address:
Azienda Agricola Forestaro, Via Pontone, 55, 80064 Sant'Agata sui Due Golfi NA, Italy

Tips for Wine Tasting in Sorrento:

- Book in advance: Many wineries prefer appointments for tours and tastings to ensure personalized attention.
- Designate a driver or use transportation services: Enjoy the wine responsibly by arranging for transportation, especially if you plan to visit multiple wineries.
- Ask questions: Take advantage of the opportunity to learn about the winemaking process, the unique characteristics of the local grapes, and the history of each winery.
- Purchase your favorites: If you discover a wine you love, consider buying a bottle or two to bring a piece of Sorrento's terroir home with you.
- Pair with local snacks: Enhance the tasting experience by trying local cheeses, cured meats, and olive oil alongside the wines.

Exploring the hills of Sorrento through a wine-tasting tour and hiking the Path of the Gods provides a dynamic and immersive way to connect with the region's natural beauty, cultural heritage, and culinary delights. Whether you're savoring the complexity of a local wine or marveling at the panoramic views from a mountain trail, Sorrento offers an unforgettable journey for the senses.

17.   Sunset   at   Punta Campanella:

Address: Punta Campanella, Massa Lubrense, 80061 Naples, Italy.

As the day draws to a close, venture to the enchanting Punta Campanella for an unforgettable sunset experience. Situated in Massa Lubrense, just a short distance from Sorrento, Punta Campanella is a captivating promontory that offers panoramic views of the Gulf of Naples. The journey to this scenic spot is an adventure in itself, with winding paths and lush landscapes providing a sense of anticipation.

Upon reaching Punta Campanella, you'll be greeted by the sight of the sun dipping below the horizon, casting a warm glow over the tranquil waters. The unobstructed vistas from this vantage point allow you to witness the sun's descent into the sea, creating a kaleidoscope of colors that paint the sky in hues of orange, pink, and gold. The sheer beauty of the scene is nothing short of magical, making it an ideal setting for a romantic and serene experience.

Punta Campanella holds historical significance as well, as it was believed to be the site of the ancient Greek temple to Athena. This adds a layer of mystique to the location, enhancing the overall atmosphere and providing a sense of connection to the past.

For the best experience, plan your visit during the late afternoon, allowing ample time to find the perfect spot to settle in and soak up the natural beauty. Whether you choose to sit on the rocks overlooking the sea or find a cozy nook amidst the flora, Punta Campanella promises a moment of tranquility and awe.

18. Handcrafted Souvenirs:

While exploring the charming streets of Sorrento, don't miss the opportunity to indulge in the town's rich tradition of crafting exquisite souvenirs. Sorrento is renowned for its skilled artisans who specialize in inlaid woodwork, ceramics, and the production of the famous limoncello. Each of these crafts reflects the unique character and history of the region, making them perfect mementos of your Sorrento visit.

Inlaid Woodwork:
Sorrento's inlaid woodwork, known as "intarsia," is a centuries-old craft that involves creating intricate designs by embedding various types of wood into a contrasting wooden surface. The result is a stunning piece of art that often depicts scenes of local landscapes, historical events, or geometric patterns. To purchase these exquisite creations, explore the numerous artisanal shops scattered throughout the historic center of Sorrento. One notable establishment is "Bottega della Tarsia Lignea" located on Via San Cesareo, where you can witness craftsmen at work and choose from a diverse array of handcrafted wooden items.

Ceramics:
Sorrento's ceramic tradition is equally impressive, with artisans producing vibrant and beautifully crafted pottery. From hand-painted plates and bowls to decorative tiles, the town's ceramic offerings capture the essence of the Mediterranean. Visit "Ceramiche Cosmolena di Margherita di Palma" on Via degli Aranci to explore a wide selection of hand-painted ceramics, each telling a unique story inspired by Sorrento's culture and natural beauty.

Limoncello:
No visit to Sorrento is complete without indulging in its famous limoncello, a lemon-flavored liqueur that embodies the essence of the region. While you can find limoncello in various stores, consider visiting one of the local limoncello factories for a more immersive experience. "Limone di

Sorrento" on Via San Cesareo is a popular choice, allowing you to witness the production process, taste different varieties, and purchase a bottle of this iconic liqueur to take home.

Corso Italia:
For a comprehensive shopping experience, take a stroll along Corso Italia, Sorrento's main street. Lined with boutiques and artisanal shops, Corso Italia offers a diverse selection of handcrafted souvenirs, allowing you to explore different styles and find the perfect keepsake. From intricately designed jewelry to handmade leather goods, the offerings along Corso Italia cater to various tastes and preferences.

Sorrento's handcrafted souvenirs are more than just tokens of your visit—they are expressions of the town's cultural identity and the craftsmanship passed down through generations. Take the time to explore the narrow streets, discover hidden workshops, and acquire pieces that will not only remind you of Sorrento but also reflect the artistry and passion of its talented artisans.

19. Local Festivals:

Sorrento's vibrant cultural scene comes alive throughout the year with a myriad of festivals and events that celebrate the town's rich history and traditions. Checking the local calendar during your visit can lead to immersive experiences, allowing you to witness traditional music, dance, and vibrant processions.

A. Feast of St. Anthony - January 17th:
The Feast of St. Anthony kicks off the year with a lively celebration in honor of the patron saint of animals. Pilgrims and locals alike gather at the Church of St. Anthony to participate in religious ceremonies, enjoy traditional

Neapolitan music, and witness a colorful procession through the streets of Sorrento.
Address: Church of St. Anthony, Via San Cesareo, Sorrento.

B. Sorrento Film Festival - Late June:
Film enthusiasts will appreciate the Sorrento Film Festival, a showcase of local and international cinema. Various venues in the town host screenings, and the festival often features discussions, workshops, and opportunities to meet filmmakers. It's a fantastic event for both cinephiles and those looking to engage with the creative arts.

Address: Multiple venues across Sorrento.

C. Sorrento Summer of Music - July to September:
Sorrento's Summer of Music is a series of concerts and performances held in iconic locations throughout the town. From classical music to contemporary performances, this event caters to a diverse range of musical tastes. Enjoy the harmonious melodies amidst the historical backdrop of Sorrento.

Address: Various locations in Sorrento.

D. Feast of Our Lady of the Assumption - August 15th:
The Feast of Our Lady of the Assumption is one of Sorrento's most significant religious celebrations. Pilgrims and locals gather for a solemn procession carrying the statue of the Virgin Mary through the streets. The event culminates in a spectacular fireworks display over the Gulf of Naples, creating a magical atmosphere.

Address: Various streets in Sorrento.

E. Sorrento Sea Festival - Early September:

As a coastal town, Sorrento pays homage to its maritime heritage with the Sorrento Sea Festival. This event features boat parades, seafood tastings, and nautical-themed activities. It's a fantastic opportunity to experience the town's deep connection to the sea and indulge in delicious fresh seafood.

Address: Marina Piccola, Sorrento.

F. Christmas Markets - December:
Sorrento transforms into a winter wonderland during the Christmas season, with charming markets lining the streets. Explore stalls selling handmade crafts, local treats, and festive decorations. The Christmas atmosphere is enhanced by seasonal performances and events, making it an enchanting time to visit.

Address: Various streets and squares in Sorrento.

These festivals provide a unique insight into Sorrento's cultural identity, allowing visitors to connect with the local community and witness the town's traditions come to life. Keep an eye on the calendar, as the dynamic events vary throughout the year, offering something for everyone.

20. Relax on Sorrento's Beaches:

Sorrento's stunning coastline beckons visitors to unwind and bask in the Mediterranean sun. Whether you prefer the lively atmosphere of Marina Piccola or the tranquility of Marina di Puolo, Sorrento's beaches offer crystal-clear waters and picturesque surroundings for a perfect day of relaxation.

A. Marina Piccola:

Nestled at the base of the cliffs below the town center, Marina Piccola is Sorrento's main beach and a bustling hub of activity. The beach is easily accessible, with a short walk from Piazza Tasso. Here, you'll find a vibrant mix of sunbathers, beachfront cafes, and water sports activities. The clear blue waters invite swimmers and snorkelers to explore the underwater beauty of the Tyrrhenian Sea.

Address: Marina Piccola, Sorrento.

B. Marina Grande:
For a more authentic and tranquil beach experience, head to Marina Grande. This charming fishing village boasts a small but picturesque beach framed by colorful buildings. The relaxed atmosphere makes it an ideal spot for a leisurely day by the sea. Enjoy fresh seafood at one of the waterfront restaurants, and take in the postcard-worthy views of fishing boats bobbing in the harbor.

Address: Marina Grande, Sorrento.

C. Puolo Beach:
Escape the crowds and discover the secluded beauty of Marina di Puolo. This beach is a hidden gem nestled in a small bay surrounded by cliffs. The calm waters and peaceful surroundings make it a perfect retreat for those seeking a more private beach experience. Several family-run seafood restaurants line the shore, offering delicious local specialties.

Address: Marina di Puolo, Sorrento.

D. Meta Beach:
Just a short drive from the town center, Meta Beach is a sandy stretch with calm waters, ideal for families and those looking for a more laid-back setting. The beach is well-equipped with facilities, including beach clubs offering

loungers and umbrellas for a comfortable day by the sea. The scenic views of the coastline add to the overall charm of Meta Beach.

Address: Meta Beach, Sorrento.

E. Regina Giovanna Beach:
For a unique beach experience, visit Regina Giovanna, a natural cove surrounded by ruins of an ancient Roman villa. The beach is accessible by a scenic walk from the town center. The historical elements combined with the azure waters create a picturesque setting for sunbathing and swimming.

Address: Regina Giovanna, Sorrento.

Whether you seek the lively atmosphere of Marina Piccola or the tranquil beauty of Marina di Puolo, Sorrento's beaches offer a variety of options for sun-soaked relaxation. Each beach has its own charm, providing visitors with a range of experiences, from vibrant beach parties to secluded retreats along the stunning Amalfi Coast.

In conclusion, Sorrento is a destination that caters to a diverse range of interests. Whether you're fascinated by history, captivated by nature, or simply seeking relaxation, Sorrento has something to offer. This guide provides a comprehensive overview of the top tourist attractions and spots, ensuring that your visit to Sorrento is filled with unforgettable experiences and cherished memories.

Chapter 3: Gastronomic Delight & Entertainment

Best local Cuisine to try out

The local cuisine in Sorrento is a delightful blend of fresh ingredients, traditional flavors, and culinary expertise. From seafood to pasta and delectable desserts, Sorrento has a diverse array of dishes that are sure to tantalize your taste buds. we'll explore the best local cuisine to try out in Sorrento, providing you with a culinary tour of this enchanting Italian town.

1. Spaghetti alle Vongole (Spaghetti with Clams):
Let's start our culinary journey with a classic seafood dish that captures the essence of Sorrento's coastal location. Spaghetti alle Vongole is a simple yet elegant dish featuring perfectly cooked spaghetti tossed with fresh clams, garlic, parsley, and a hint of white wine. The briny flavors of the clams combined with the aromatic garlic create a symphony of tastes that is both refreshing and satisfying.

2. Gnocchi alla Sorrentina:
For a taste of comfort food with a Sorrento twist, try Gnocchi alla Sorrentina. These potato dumplings are typically baked with tomato sauce, fresh mozzarella, and basil. The result is a dish that's rich, cheesy, and irresistibly delicious. The soft pillows of gnocchi absorb the flavors of the sauce, creating a mouthwatering experience that's hard to forget.

3. Limoncello:
Sorrento is famous for its lemons, and one of the best ways to experience their vibrant flavor is through Limoncello. This traditional Italian lemon liqueur is made by steeping lemon zest in alcohol and then sweetening the infusion with sugar.

The result is a bright, citrusy liqueur that serves as the perfect digestif. Be sure to indulge in a glass of Limoncello after your meal to cleanse your palate and savor the taste of Sorrento's iconic lemons.

4. Ravioli Capresi:
Ravioli Capresi is a unique local dish that showcases the culinary creativity of Sorrento. These ravioli are filled with caciotta cheese, marjoram, and a hint of grated lemon zest. The dish is then topped with a simple tomato sauce, allowing the delicate flavors of the filling to shine. The combination of creamy cheese, aromatic herbs, and citrusy zest makes Ravioli Capresi a must-try for those seeking a distinctive Sorrento dining experience.

5. Frittura di Paranza (Mixed Seafood Fry):
Seafood lovers rejoice! Frittura di Paranza is a delectable platter of mixed seafood, including small fish, shrimp, and calamari, all lightly battered and fried to perfection. This dish embodies the essence of Sorrento's coastal cuisine, highlighting the freshness and quality of the seafood sourced from the nearby Mediterranean waters. Squeeze a bit of lemon over the crispy morsels for an extra burst of flavor.

6. Sfogliatella:
No culinary exploration of Sorrento is complete without indulging in a Sfogliatella. This iconic pastry is a delightful combination of thin layers of dough filled with ricotta cheese, citrus peel, and a hint of cinnamon. The result is a flaky, sweet treat that showcases the region's expertise in pastry making. Whether you choose the riccia (curly) or frolla (shortcrust) variation, Sfogliatella is a must-have dessert in Sorrento.

7. Melanzane alla Parmigiana (Eggplant Parmesan):

While Melanzane alla Parmigiana is not exclusive to Sorrento, the local rendition of this classic Italian dish is a standout. Layers of thinly sliced, fried eggplant are stacked with tomato sauce and melted mozzarella, creating a hearty and flavorful casserole. The eggplant in Sorrento benefits from the region's fertile soil, resulting in a dish that highlights the natural sweetness and tenderness of this versatile vegetable.

8. Pizza Margherita:
No visit to Italy is complete without savoring a traditional Neapolitan pizza, and Sorrento is no exception. The birthplace of pizza is just a short drive away, and Sorrento's pizzerias uphold the same standards of excellence. Try the Pizza Margherita, a classic topped with tomato, mozzarella, fresh basil, and a drizzle of olive oil. The simplicity of the ingredients allows the quality of each component to shine, making every bite a true taste of Italy.

9. Linguine al Limone (Lemon Linguine):
Building on Sorrento's love affair with lemons, Linguine al Limone is a pasta dish that celebrates the bright and zesty flavors of this citrus fruit. The pasta is coated in a velvety sauce made with lemon juice, zest, butter, and Parmesan cheese. The result is a refreshing and indulgent dish that perfectly captures the essence of Sorrento's culinary scene.

10. Baba au Rhum:
To cap off your culinary journey in Sorrento, treat yourself to a Baba au Rhum, a delightful dessert that showcases the town's French influence. This small, yeast-risen cake is soaked in a rum-infused syrup, giving it a moist and flavorful profile. Often topped with whipped cream or pastry cream, Baba au Rhum is a sweet conclusion to your exploration of Sorrento's diverse and delicious cuisine.

11. Caprese Salad:

Sorrento's version of the classic Caprese Salad is a testament to the region's commitment to using top-quality ingredients. Fresh, ripe tomatoes, buffalo mozzarella, basil leaves, and a drizzle of extra virgin olive oil come together to create a refreshing and visually stunning salad. The sweetness of the tomatoes and the creaminess of the mozzarella make this dish a perfect starter or light lunch option.

12. Sartù di Riso:

Sartù di Riso is a hearty and flavorful rice dish that originated in the Campania region, and Sorrento has its own delicious variation. This baked rice casserole is typically filled with a rich mixture of sausage, peas, mushrooms, and a tomato-based sauce. The rice absorbs the savory flavors during baking, resulting in a comforting and satisfying one-dish meal that reflects the heartiness of Sorrento's cuisine.

13. Scialatielli ai Frutti di Mare:

Seafood takes center stage once again with Scialatielli ai Frutti di Mare, a pasta dish that combines the chewy goodness of scialatielli pasta with an array of fresh seafood. Mussels, clams, shrimp, and calamari are sautéed with garlic, tomatoes, and white wine to create a flavorful sauce that perfectly complements the homemade pasta. This dish is a celebration of Sorrento's maritime bounty.

14. Aglianico Wine:

To complement your culinary experience in Sorrento, be sure to explore the local wines. Aglianico, a red wine grape variety native to southern Italy, produces robust and full-bodied wines. The volcanic soils of the Campania region impart unique characteristics to the Aglianico wines, making them a perfect accompaniment to the rich flavors of Sorrento's cuisine. Sip on a glass of Aglianico and savor the terroir of the region.

15. Anchovies from Cetara:
While not technically a Sorrento dish, the nearby fishing village of Cetara produces some of the best anchovies in the region. These small, flavorful fish are typically preserved in salt and then used in various dishes to add a burst of umami. Try them in a simple pasta dish or on a pizza for a taste of the authentic local flavors.

16. Insalata di Mare (Seafood Salad):
Insalata di Mare is a refreshing seafood salad that highlights the bounty of the Mediterranean. Mixed seafood, such as octopus, shrimp, and squid, is marinated with olive oil, lemon juice, and fresh herbs. The result is a light and tangy salad that showcases the quality and freshness of the seafood available in Sorrento.

17. Paccheri alla Nerano:
Paccheri alla Nerano is a pasta dish that originated in the nearby town of Nerano but has become a beloved staple in Sorrento's culinary scene. Paccheri, large tube-shaped pasta, is tossed with a creamy sauce made from provolone del Monaco cheese and zucchini. The combination of the rich cheese and the sweetness of the zucchini creates a pasta dish that is both indulgent and comforting.

18. Zuppa di Pesce (Fish Soup):
For a taste of the sea in a comforting and aromatic broth, try Zuppa di Pesce. This fish soup features a medley of fresh fish, shellfish, tomatoes, and herbs, creating a flavorful and soul-warming dish. The broth is often infused with a touch of white wine and garlic, adding depth to the seafood flavors. Pair it with a crusty piece of Italian bread to soak up every delicious drop.

19. Babà al Limoncello:
Building on the popularity of Limoncello, Sorrento puts a twist on the traditional Baba au Rhum with Babà al Limoncello. These small, yeast-risen cakes are soaked in a syrup made with the iconic lemon liqueur, imparting a citrusy kick to the dessert. Topped with a dollop of whipped cream or served with fresh berries, Babà al Limoncello is a delightful way to end your meal on a sweet note.

20. Cannoli:
No culinary journey is complete without a taste of Italy's beloved dessert, and Sorrento's Cannoli is a treat not to be missed. Crispy, fried pastry tubes are filled with a sweet and creamy ricotta filling, often studded with candied fruit or chocolate chips. The combination of the crunchy shell and luscious filling makes Cannoli a satisfying and iconic dessert that perfectly encapsulates the sweet side of Sorrento.

As you explore the diverse and delicious cuisine of Sorrento, these additional examples will surely enhance your culinary adventure. From seafood delights to comforting pasta dishes and irresistible desserts, Sorrento's local fare is a celebration of the region's rich culinary heritage. Buon viaggio gastronomico!

Best Local Drinks to try Out
While the breathtaking landscapes are a major draw, Sorrento also boasts a rich culinary tradition, including a variety of delightful local drinks. From traditional liqueurs to refreshing fruit-based beverages, Sorrento offers a diverse array of drinks that cater to every taste. we'll explore the best local drinks to try out in Sorrento, providing a comprehensive overview of the flavors that define this picturesque region.

Limoncello: The Citrus Jewel of Sorrento
One cannot delve into Sorrento's local drinks without mentioning Limoncello, the region's most iconic beverage. Sorrento is famous for its lemons, and Limoncello perfectly captures the essence of these vibrant citrus fruits. This sweet and tangy liqueur is made by infusing lemon zest into alcohol, creating a refreshing and aromatic drink. The bright yellow color and intense lemon flavor make Limoncello a favorite among locals and tourists alike. It is often served chilled as a digestif, providing a perfect conclusion to a delicious meal.

Nocino: A Walnut-infused Elixir
Nocino is a unique liqueur that highlights the flavors of green walnuts. This dark and complex drink is crafted by macerating unripe walnuts in alcohol and adding a blend of spices. The result is a rich, bittersweet liqueur that showcases the earthy notes of the walnuts. Nocino is traditionally enjoyed as a digestif and is often served neat or over ice. Its distinctive flavor profile sets it apart from other Italian liqueurs, making it a must-try for those seeking a taste of Sorrento's artisanal beverages.

Taralli e Latte: A Twist on the Classic Milk and Cookies
For a non-alcoholic option that still captures the essence of Sorrento, try Taralli e Latte. This simple yet satisfying drink consists of Taralli, a type of Italian snack cracker, paired with a glass of fresh milk. The Taralli, often flavored with fennel or black pepper, adds a crunchy element to the creamy milk. This combination is a beloved local tradition, enjoyed as a light breakfast or afternoon snack. It provides a glimpse into the everyday flavors that characterize Sorrento's culinary scene.

Granita al Limone: Cool and Refreshing

Sorrento's warm climate calls for refreshing beverages, and Granita al Limone fits the bill perfectly. This frozen dessert is a delightful blend of crushed ice, fresh lemon juice, and sugar. The result is a slushy concoction that captures the essence of Sorrento's lemons in a cool and invigorating form. Granita al Limone is often enjoyed during hot summer days, providing a sweet respite from the sun. Its icy texture and zesty flavor make it a favorite among locals and visitors seeking a delightful way to stay cool.

Aglianico del Taburno: A Local Wine Gem
While Sorrento is not primarily known for its wines, the nearby region of Campania boasts some exceptional varieties. One such wine to explore is Aglianico del Taburno. This red wine, made from the Aglianico grape, is known for its bold and robust character. With deep red color and complex aromas of dark fruits and spices, Aglianico del Taburno pairs wonderfully with the rich and savory dishes found in Sorrento. Whether you're a wine enthusiast or a casual drinker, exploring the local wine scene adds another layer to Sorrento's diverse beverage offerings.

Limoncello Spritz: A Modern Twist on Tradition
For a contemporary take on the classic Limoncello, try a Limoncello Spritz. This refreshing cocktail combines Limoncello with sparkling water and a splash of prosecco. The result is a light and effervescent drink that retains the vibrant lemon flavors while adding a bubbly twist. The Limoncello Spritz is a popular choice for a pre-dinner aperitif, providing a lively and sociable start to the evening. Sip on this modern creation while enjoying the sunset over the Bay of Naples for an authentic Sorrento experience.

Sfusato Amalfitano: The Lemon of Sorrento
To truly appreciate Sorrento's lemons, savor the Sfusato Amalfitano, a type of lemon that is indigenous to the region.

Known for its elongated shape and intense aroma, this lemon variety is a key ingredient in many local dishes and beverages. The Sfusato Amalfitano is not only a culinary treasure but also a symbol of Sorrento's agricultural heritage. Whether enjoyed in a refreshing drink, used in cooking, or simply as a fragrant centerpiece, the Sfusato Amalfitano is a testament to the unique flavors that define Sorrento.

Caffè del Nonno: A Sweet Coffee Tradition
Coffee holds a special place in Italian culture, and Sorrento is no exception. For a local coffee experience, try Caffè del Nonno, a traditional coffee preparation that adds a sweet twist to your caffeine fix. This coffee is made by combining espresso with a touch of sugar and lemon zest, creating a unique flavor profile that balances the bitterness of the coffee with the sweetness of the sugar and the citrusy notes of the lemon. Caffè del Nonno is a delightful way to start your day or to indulge in a sweet afternoon pick-me-up.

Baba al Limoncello: A Boozy Dessert Delight
For those with a sweet tooth, Baba al Limoncello is a decadent dessert that combines the rich flavors of the iconic Limoncello with a soft and sponge-like cake. Babà, a small yeast cake, is soaked in a Limoncello-infused syrup, resulting in a moist and flavorful treat. This dessert is a favorite in Sorrento's pastry shops and is often enjoyed with a cup of coffee or as a sweet ending to a leisurely meal. Indulge in the luscious combination of citrus and cake, and you'll understand why Baba al Limoncello is a beloved local delicacy.

Limoncello Sorbet: A Frozen Delight
To cap off our exploration of Sorrento's local drinks, indulge in the cool and creamy goodness of Limoncello Sorbet. This frozen dessert takes the essence of Limoncello and transforms it into a refreshing and tangy sorbet. The velvety

texture and intense lemon flavor make this sorbet a delightful way to cleanse your palate and satisfy your sweet cravings. Whether enjoyed on its own or as a palate cleanser between courses, Limoncello Sorbet captures the essence of Sorrento's flavors in a frozen delight.

In conclusion, Sorrento's local drinks offer a diverse and flavorful journey through the region's culinary heritage. From the iconic Limoncello to the rich and complex Nocino, each beverage tells a story of Sorrento's unique ingredients and traditions. Whether you prefer the tangy notes of citrus, the robust character of local wines, or the sweet indulgence of dessert drinks, Sorrento has something to offer every palate. So, as you explore this picturesque coastal town, be sure to raise a glass and savor the authentic flavors that make Sorrento a true culinary gem on the Italian coast.

Top Restaurant

Ristorante Piazza Tasso
Address: Piazza Tasso, 34, 80067 Sorrento NA, Italy

Ristorante Piazza Tasso is a charming restaurant located right in the heart of Sorrento's historic center, overlooking the bustling Piazza Tasso. Known for its authentic Italian cuisine and warm ambiance, this restaurant is a favorite among locals and tourists alike.

The menu at Ristorante Piazza Tasso features a delightful selection of traditional dishes made with fresh, locally sourced ingredients. From classic pasta dishes to mouthwatering seafood specialties, every item on the menu is a celebration of the rich flavors of Italian gastronomy.

The cozy interior of the restaurant is complemented by attentive and friendly staff, creating a welcoming atmosphere for diners. Whether you choose to sit indoors or on the outdoor terrace, you'll be treated to a memorable dining experience with stunning views of the lively square.

Il Buco
Address: Via S. Antonino, 2, 80067 Sorrento NA, Italy

Nestled in a charming alley just a short walk from the main square, Il Buco is a hidden gem that captures the essence of Sorrento's culinary scene. This family-run restaurant is renowned for its dedication to traditional recipes passed down through generations.

The menu at Il Buco is a testament to the restaurant's commitment to using the finest local ingredients. Guests can savor the flavors of homemade pasta, freshly caught seafood, and mouthwatering desserts that showcase the expertise of the kitchen.

The rustic and intimate ambiance adds to the overall charm of Il Buco, making it an ideal spot for a romantic dinner or a family gathering. Don't forget to explore the extensive wine list featuring both local and international selections to complement your meal.

L'Antica Trattoria
Address: Via Fuoro, 23, 80067 Sorrento NA, Italy

For a truly authentic dining experience, L'Antica Trattoria is a must-visit destination in Sorrento. Tucked away from the bustling crowds, this trattoria exudes a rustic charm that transports diners to a bygone era of Italian hospitality.

The menu at L'Antica Trattoria showcases a variety of regional specialties, with an emphasis on simplicity and quality. From handmade pastas to flavorful meat dishes, each plate is a celebration of the local culinary heritage. The chefs take pride in sourcing ingredients from nearby markets, ensuring a farm-to-table experience for patrons.

The interior of L'Antica Trattoria is adorned with vintage decor, creating a cozy and nostalgic atmosphere. Whether you're a connoisseur of Italian cuisine or a first-time visitor, this trattoria offers a memorable journey through the flavors of Sorrento.

Terrazza Bosquet
Address: Via Luigi De Maio, 35, 80067 Sorrento NA, Italy

Perched on the heights of Sorrento, Terrazza Bosquet offers not only exquisite cuisine but also breathtaking panoramic views of the Bay of Naples. This Michelin-starred restaurant combines culinary excellence with a stunning backdrop, creating a dining experience that is nothing short of spectacular.

The menu at Terrazza Bosquet is a fusion of contemporary flair and traditional flavors. The chefs artfully present dishes that showcase the region's bounty, from fresh seafood to seasonal vegetables. The extensive wine list features carefully curated selections to complement the diverse menu.

The terrace, after which the restaurant is named, provides an elegant setting for al fresco dining. Whether you're enjoying a leisurely lunch or a romantic dinner, Terrazza Bosquet promises an unforgettable gastronomic journey with the added bonus of unparalleled views.

Soul & Fish
Address: Via Marina Grande, 10, 80067 Sorrento NA, Italy

If you're seeking a seafood-centric dining experience with a contemporary twist, Soul & Fish is the place to be. Situated near the picturesque Marina Grande, this restaurant combines the freshest catches with innovative culinary techniques, creating a seafood lover's paradise.

The menu at Soul & Fish features a variety of dishes that highlight the natural flavors of the sea. From creative seafood platters to perfectly grilled fish, each offering is a testament to the restaurant's commitment to quality and flavor. Vegetarian options are also available for those looking for a diverse dining experience.

The modern and stylish interior of Soul & Fish adds a touch of sophistication to the overall ambiance. With its prime location and culinary expertise, this restaurant has become a go-to destination for those seeking a contemporary take on Sorrento's maritime culinary traditions.

Sorrento offers a diverse range of dining experiences, from historic trattorias to Michelin-starred gems. Whether you're a fan of traditional Italian fare or crave a more contemporary culinary adventure, these top restaurants in Sorrento are sure to satisfy your palate. So, take a stroll through the charming streets of Sorrento and indulge in the rich flavors that this picturesque Italian town has to offer.

Best bar in the city

Whether you're looking for a cozy spot to enjoy a glass of local wine or a lively bar to dance the night away, Sorrento has something for everyone. In this guide, we'll explore some of the best bars in Sorrento, each offering a unique experience and a taste of the local culture.

1. Fauno Bar

Address: Via Fuorimura, 5, 80067 Sorrento NA, Italy

Nestled in the heart of Sorrento's historic center, Fauno Bar is a classic Italian bar known for its laid-back atmosphere and extensive cocktail menu. The bartenders here are true mixology experts, creating delicious concoctions that range from traditional Negronis to innovative, signature drinks. With outdoor seating available, Fauno Bar is an ideal spot to enjoy your drinks while soaking in the charming ambiance of Sorrento.

2. Africana Famous Club

Address: Via del Capo, 11, 80067 Massa Lubrense NA, Italy

For those seeking a unique and unforgettable nightlife experience, Africana Famous Club is a must-visit. Located in a natural cave overlooking the sea, this iconic club has been a hotspot for locals and tourists alike since the 1960s. Dance the night away to a mix of international and local beats while enjoying the cool sea breeze. The entrance fee includes a welcome drink, making it a fantastic value for a night of entertainment.

3. Bar Syrenuse

Address: Piazza Tasso, 34, 80067 Sorrento NA, Italy

Situated in the bustling Piazza Tasso, Bar Syrenuse is a trendy cocktail bar that combines a modern vibe with a touch of Sorrento's traditional charm. The bar offers a wide selection of craft cocktails, and the skilled bartenders are always eager to recommend their favorites. The stylish interior and lively atmosphere make Bar Syrenuse a popular choice for both locals and visitors looking to start their evening with a bang.

4. Marameo Beach

Address: Via del Mare, 30, 80067 Sorrento NA, Italy

For those who prefer a beachfront setting, Marameo Beach is the perfect destination. This laid-back bar offers a relaxed atmosphere with stunning views of the Gulf of Naples. Sink your toes into the sand as you sip on refreshing cocktails crafted with locally sourced ingredients. Marameo Beach is not only a great spot for daytime relaxation but also transforms into a lively beach club as the sun sets, with live music and DJ performances.

5. Wine & More

Address: Corso Italia, 55, 80067 Sorrento NA, Italy

If you're a wine enthusiast, Wine & More is a must-visit destination in Sorrento. This elegant wine bar boasts an extensive selection of local and international wines, expertly curated to satisfy even the most discerning palates. The knowledgeable staff can guide you through the menu, helping you discover new and exciting flavors. Pair your wine with a selection of artisanal cheeses and cured meats for a truly indulgent experience.

6. Foreigner's Club

Address: Via Luigi De Maio, 35, 80067 Sorrento NA, Italy

Perched on a cliff overlooking the Gulf of Naples, the Foreigner's Club is a historic establishment with a captivating atmosphere. This exclusive club offers a sophisticated setting for those looking to enjoy panoramic views while sipping on expertly crafted cocktails. The classic decor and attentive service make it a favorite among both locals and tourists seeking an upscale and memorable evening in Sorrento.

7. Sedil Dominova

Address: Largo Arcivescovado, 4, 80067 Sorrento NA, Italy

For a taste of Sorrento's history and culture, head to Sedil Dominova. This traditional Italian bar is located in a historic building that once served as a meeting place for the city's noble families. Today, it retains its historic charm while offering a diverse menu of drinks. From classic Italian aperitivos to modern craft cocktails, Sedil Dominova provides a unique and atmospheric setting to enjoy the rich flavors of Sorrento.

8. Aurora Bar

Address: Via Fuorimura, 7, 80067 Sorrento NA, Italy

Located just a short walk from the Piazza Tasso, Aurora Bar is a hidden gem known for its welcoming atmosphere and extensive drink selection. The bar's outdoor terrace provides a cozy spot to unwind with a cocktail after a day of exploring Sorrento. With a menu that includes both classic and innovative drinks, Aurora Bar caters to a diverse range of tastes, making it a popular choice for locals and tourists alike.

9. Bar Rita

Address: Via degli Aranci, 10, 80067 Sorrento NA, Italy

If you're in the mood for a lively and colorful atmosphere, Bar Rita is the place to be. This vibrant bar, adorned with eclectic decor and fairy lights, exudes a fun and energetic vibe. Known for its creative cocktails and friendly staff, Bar Rita is a favorite among the younger crowd. Whether you're looking to dance to the latest tunes or simply enjoy a casual drink with friends, Bar Rita offers a dynamic and memorable experience.

10. Bellevue Syrene Bar

Address: Piazza della Vittoria, 5, 80067 Sorrento NA, Italy

For a touch of luxury and elegance, head to Bellevue Syrene Bar. Situated in the prestigious Bellevue Syrene Hotel, this bar offers breathtaking views of the Gulf of Naples from its terrace. The sophisticated ambiance, coupled with an extensive menu of premium cocktails, makes it a top choice for those seeking a refined and intimate setting. Whether you're celebrating a special occasion or simply want to indulge in a night of opulence, Bellevue Syrene Bar delivers a memorable experience.

Conclusion

Sorrento's diverse and vibrant bar scene caters to a wide range of tastes and preferences. Whether you prefer a beachfront setting, a historic atmosphere, or a trendy cocktail bar, Sorrento has it all. From the iconic Africana Famous Club to the charming Sedil Dominova, each bar on this list offers a unique glimpse into the rich culture and lively spirit of this coastal town. So, grab your friends, explore the streets of Sorrento, and immerse yourself in the unforgettable nightlife this Italian gem has to offer. Cheers!

Best Nightclub in the city

1. Fauno Notte Club
Address: Via dell'Accademia, 12, 80067 Sorrento NA, Italy

Fauno Notte Club is a prominent nightlife destination in Sorrento, known for its energetic atmosphere and top-notch music. Located in the heart of the city, this club attracts both locals and tourists looking for a memorable night out. The interior boasts modern decor, state-of-the-art lighting, and a spacious dance floor.

The club hosts a variety of events throughout the week, featuring talented DJs playing a mix of electronic, house, and chart-topping hits. Whether you're into dancing the night away or simply enjoying great music with friends, Fauno Notte Club offers an unforgettable experience.

Additionally, the club has a well-stocked bar serving a wide range of cocktails and beverages. The attentive staff ensures that your night is filled with great music, fantastic drinks, and a lively crowd.

2. Maré Club
Address: Via Correale, 25, 80067 Sorrento NA, Italy

Maré Club is a beachfront nightclub in Sorrento, providing a unique and refreshing experience. With its stunning views of the Tyrrhenian Sea, this venue combines the excitement of a nightclub with the relaxed vibe of a beach club.

The club is known for its themed parties, live performances, and a diverse music selection. Whether you prefer electronic beats, Latin rhythms, or classic hits, Maré Club caters to various tastes. The outdoor seating area allows guests to enjoy the cool sea breeze while sipping on signature cocktails.

Maré Club often collaborates with renowned DJs and hosts special events, making it a hotspot for those seeking a dynamic and stylish nightlife experience. Keep an eye on their event calendar for upcoming parties and performances.

3. Syrenuse Bar & Lounge
Address: Piazza Tasso, 34, 80067 Sorrento NA, Italy

Syrenuse Bar & Lounge offers a sophisticated and upscale nightlife experience in the heart of Sorrento. Nestled in Piazza Tasso, this venue is not only a nightclub but also a chic lounge where patrons can unwind in style.

The interior exudes elegance with plush seating, ambient lighting, and a well-curated selection of music. Syrenuse Bar & Lounge is known for its expertly crafted cocktails, featuring both classic and innovative concoctions. The skilled bartenders are dedicated to providing a personalized and memorable drinking experience.

The club often hosts live music performances, creating a refined atmosphere for guests to enjoy. If you're looking for a more laid-back yet sophisticated night out, Syrenuse Bar & Lounge is the perfect destination.

4. Plaza Disco Club
Address: Via degli Aranci, 75, 80067 Sorrento NA, Italy

For those seeking a high-energy and lively nightclub experience, Plaza Disco Club is a must-visit destination in Sorrento. Situated on Via degli Aranci, this club is known for its pulsating beats, neon lights, and a bustling dance floor.

Plaza Disco Club features a diverse lineup of DJs playing everything from EDM to hip-hop, ensuring there's something for everyone. The club's vibrant atmosphere and friendly crowd make it a favorite among locals and visitors alike.

The club often hosts themed nights and special events, adding an extra layer of excitement to the already dynamic atmosphere. If you're in the mood for an exhilarating night of dancing and celebration, Plaza Disco Club is the place to be.

5. Liquid Sky
Address: Via Marina Piccola, 5, 80067 Sorrento NA, Italy

Liquid Sky is a unique nightclub located near the Marina Piccola, offering a one-of-a-kind experience that combines music, art, and technology. The club's interior is adorned with immersive light installations, creating a futuristic and captivating environment.

Known for its cutting-edge electronic music scene, Liquid Sky attracts a diverse crowd of music enthusiasts. The club frequently hosts international and local DJs, pushing the boundaries of sonic exploration.

The bar at Liquid Sky is stocked with a wide range of spirits and innovative cocktails, ensuring that your taste buds are as stimulated as your senses. With its avant-garde approach to nightlife, Liquid Sky stands out as a must-visit destination for those looking for a truly unique and unforgettable experience.

Sorrento's nightlife scene offers a diverse range of options for those looking to dance the night away, enjoy live music, or simply unwind in a stylish setting. From beachfront clubs with scenic views to upscale lounges and high-energy discos, Sorrento has something for every taste.

Before heading out, it's recommended to check the current schedules, events, and any COVID-19 related restrictions that may impact the operation of these nightclubs. Now, armed with this guide, go ahead and explore the best of Sorrento's nightlife scene for an unforgettable evening in this picturesque Italian coastal town.

Chapter 4: Travel Itineraries

Outdoor adventure itinerary

Creating a comprehensive outdoor adventure itinerary for Sorrento is like laying out a buffet of excitement. From breathtaking landscapes to adrenaline-pumping activities, Sorrento offers a plethora of experiences that cater to every adventurer's appetite. So, buckle up and get ready for an unforgettable journey filled with nature, thrills, and cultural exploration.

Day 1: Arrival and Acquaintance with Sorrento

Morning: Arrival in Sorrento
Start your adventure by arriving in the charming town of Sorrento. Whether you choose to arrive by plane, train, or car, the journey itself sets the stage for the excitement that lies ahead. Once you've settled into your accommodation, take a leisurely stroll around the town to get a feel for its unique blend of history and modernity.

Afternoon: Cliffside Views at Villa Comunale
For a panoramic introduction to Sorrento, head to Villa Comunale, a beautiful park perched on the cliffs overlooking the Bay of Naples. The stunning views of Mount Vesuvius and the Gulf of Naples make it an ideal spot for a peaceful afternoon. Take a moment to breathe in the fresh sea air and snap some photos to remember the beginning of your adventure.

Evening: Taste of Sorrento's Cuisine
Sorrento is not only a feast for the eyes but also for the taste buds. Head to a local trattoria to savor some traditional

dishes, such as gnocchi alla sorrentina or fresh seafood pasta. Pair your meal with a glass of limoncello, the famous lemon liqueur that is a specialty of the region.

Day 2: Hiking the Path of the Gods

Morning: Breakfast with a View
Start your day with a hearty breakfast, fueling up for the day's adventure. Choose a café with a view of the sea or the town, and enjoy the Mediterranean charm that surrounds you.

Late Morning to Afternoon: Path of the Gods Hike
Embark on a thrilling hike along the Sentiero degli Dei, or the Path of the Gods. This famous trail offers breathtaking views of the Amalfi Coast, with rugged cliffs plunging into the azure sea. The trail takes you through quaint villages and provides ample opportunities to capture the stunning scenery. Remember to pack water, sunscreen, and sturdy hiking shoes for this awe-inspiring journey.

Evening: Sunset in Positano
After completing the hike, reward yourself with a visit to the picturesque town of Positano. Known for its colorful buildings cascading down the cliffside, Positano is a postcard-perfect destination. Spend the evening exploring the narrow streets, shopping for local crafts, and enjoying a seaside dinner as the sun sets over the Tyrrhenian Sea.

Day 3: Water Adventures and Historical Exploration

Morning: Kayaking along the Sorrento Coast
For a dose of adrenaline, kick off your day with a kayaking adventure along the Sorrento Coast. Paddle through crystal-clear waters, explore hidden sea caves, and marvel at the

marine life beneath you. Several local operators offer guided kayak tours, ensuring a safe and exhilarating experience.

Afternoon: Historical Exploration in Pompeii

After drying off from your morning adventure, delve into history with a visit to the ancient city of Pompeii. Just a short drive from Sorrento, Pompeii offers a fascinating glimpse into daily life during the Roman Empire. Wander through the well-preserved ruins, marvel at the ancient architecture, and imagine the bustling streets that once thrived with activity.

Evening: Dinner in the Old Town

Return to Sorrento for a relaxing evening in the Old Town. Explore the charming alleyways, visit local shops, and indulge in a delicious dinner at one of the many trattorias or ristorantes. Sorrento's Old Town comes alive in the evening, with a vibrant atmosphere that invites you to immerse yourself in the local culture.

Day 4: Sailing the Mediterranean

Morning: Explore Capri

Embark on a ferry or private boat to the enchanting island of Capri. Known for its stunning Blue Grotto and lush landscapes, Capri is a playground for outdoor enthusiasts. Spend the morning exploring the island's natural wonders, from the dramatic Faraglioni rock formations to the pristine beaches.

Afternoon: Snorkeling and Relaxation

Take advantage of the clear waters surrounding Capri with an afternoon of snorkeling. Discover the vibrant marine life and underwater caves, or simply relax on a secluded beach. The Mediterranean Sea provides the perfect backdrop for a leisurely afternoon, allowing you to unwind and soak in the beauty of your surroundings.

Evening: Sunset Sail Back to Sorrento
As the day winds down, board a sunset cruise back to Sorrento. Enjoy the breathtaking views of the coastline bathed in the warm hues of the setting sun. This serene journey caps off your day of island exploration and sets the stage for a relaxing evening in Sorrento.

Day 5: Culinary Delights and Departure

Morning: Cooking Class
Immerse yourself in Sorrento's culinary traditions with a morning cooking class. Learn the secrets of crafting authentic Italian dishes, using fresh, locally sourced ingredients. From homemade pasta to traditional desserts, this hands-on experience provides a delicious way to connect with the local culture.

Afternoon: Last-minute Explorations
Before bidding farewell to Sorrento, take some time for last-minute explorations. Visit any attractions you may have missed, pick up souvenirs, or simply savor a leisurely stroll through the town's charming streets. Sorrento's laid-back atmosphere encourages you to embrace the slow pace and appreciate the beauty of the moment.

Evening: Farewell Dinner
Conclude your outdoor adventure in Sorrento with a farewell dinner at a waterfront restaurant. Reflect on the memories you've created, savor the flavors of the region one last time, and toast to the success of your unforgettable journey. Sorrento's warm hospitality and breathtaking landscapes ensure that your outdoor adventure will be etched in your memory for years to come.

As you bid adieu to Sorrento, take with you not just memories of thrilling activities and scenic vistas, but also a sense of the region's rich history, vibrant culture, and the warmth of its people. Whether you're a nature lover, history buff, or adrenaline seeker, Sorrento offers a diverse range of experiences that cater to every adventurer's soul.

Romantic itinerary

Planning a romantic itinerary in Sorrento can be an enchanting experience, filled with breathtaking views, delectable cuisine, and unforgettable moments. Whether you're a couple seeking adventure, relaxation, or a perfect blend of both, Sorrento offers a plethora of activities to make your romantic getaway truly special. Let's dive into a detailed itinerary that spans the best of Sorrento's romantic offerings.

Day 1: Arrival and Sunset Stroll

Morning:
Arrive in Sorrento and check into your chosen accommodation, whether it's a charming boutique hotel or a cozy bed and breakfast. Freshen up and get ready for a delightful day ahead.

Afternoon:
Start your romantic journey with a leisurely lunch at a local trattoria. Indulge in authentic Italian flavors, including freshly made pasta, seafood, and local wines. After lunch, take a stroll through Sorrento's historic center, exploring narrow cobblestone streets lined with shops selling handmade crafts, limoncello, and local delicacies.

Evening:
As the sun begins to set, head to Villa Comunale, a beautiful park offering panoramic views of the Gulf of Naples and Mount Vesuvius. Find a quiet spot to relax and enjoy the mesmerizing sunset with your loved one. Capture the

moment with photos or simply immerse yourselves in the romantic atmosphere.

Dinner:
Choose a romantic restaurant with a terrace overlooking the sea. Savour traditional Italian dishes, paired with a fine local wine. Let the candlelight and sea breeze enhance the magic of your evening.

Day 2: Boat Excursion to Capri

Morning:
Kick off your day with a delicious Italian breakfast at a local café. Fuel up for a day of adventure with freshly brewed coffee, pastries, and fresh fruits.

Late Morning - Afternoon:
Embark on a boat excursion to the enchanting island of Capri. Whether you opt for a private boat or a group tour, exploring the crystal-clear waters surrounding Capri is a romantic experience. Visit the famous Blue Grotto, take a dip in the turquoise sea, and enjoy the stunning coastal scenery.

Lunch on Capri:
Dine in one of Capri's waterfront restaurants, savoring the island's specialties. Fresh seafood, Mediterranean salads, and homemade gelato are among the delectable options.

Evening:
Return to Sorrento in the late afternoon and relax at your accommodation. Freshen up before heading out for an evening passeggiata, a leisurely stroll through the town. Explore Sorrento by night, with its charmingly lit streets and lively atmosphere.

Dinner:
Choose a romantic restaurant with a terrace overlooking the sea or the town. Enjoy a romantic dinner with local dishes and a glass of limoncello to cap off your day.

Day 3: Cooking Class and Wine Tasting

Morning:
Start your day with a leisurely breakfast and plan for a morning cooking class. Engage in a hands-on experience, learning to prepare traditional Italian dishes with your partner. This immersive activity not only adds a fun element to your trip but also provides you with skills to recreate these dishes at home.

Afternoon:
After your cooking class, explore Sorrento's local markets or take a relaxing stroll through the citrus groves. Alternatively, visit a local winery for a wine-tasting session. Savor the flavors of the region, from crisp whites to robust reds, and enjoy the picturesque vineyard setting.

Evening:
Indulge in a romantic dinner at a Michelin-starred restaurant or a hidden gem known for its local specialties. Share the dishes you've learned to prepare earlier in the day and relish the flavors of your culinary creations.

Day 4: Amalfi Coast Excursion

Morning:
Wake up to another delightful day in Sorrento and enjoy a leisurely breakfast. Today, embark on a scenic drive along the Amalfi Coast, one of Italy's most iconic coastal routes. The breathtaking views of the rugged cliffs and azure sea provide a perfect backdrop for your romantic escapade.

Afternoon:
Stop in picturesque towns like Positano and Amalfi, exploring charming streets, visiting local shops, and savoring coastal delicacies. Take a boat tour along the coast to fully appreciate the stunning landscape and the charm of the Amalfi villages from the water.

Lunch on the Amalfi Coast:
Dine in one of the seaside restaurants, enjoying fresh seafood and regional specialties while taking in panoramic views.

Evening:
Return to Sorrento in the late afternoon and spend the evening at leisure. You may choose to relax at a spa, take a romantic evening stroll, or simply unwind at a cozy café.

Day 5: Relaxation and Departure

Morning:
On your final day, take it slow and enjoy a leisurely morning. Have a late breakfast at your accommodation or venture to a local café for a relaxing start to the day.

Midday:
If you haven't already, explore Sorrento's beaches for a few hours of sun and sea. Alternatively, visit a local spa for a couples' massage or a rejuvenating wellness experience.

Afternoon:
For your last lunch in Sorrento, choose a beachfront restaurant or a quaint trattoria to savor the final tastes of the Amalfi Coast.

Evening:
As the day draws to a close, reminisce about the wonderful moments you've shared in Sorrento. Enjoy a farewell dinner

at a romantic spot, perhaps with live music or a captivating view.

Conclusion:
Sorrento's romantic itinerary offers a perfect blend of adventure, relaxation, and culinary delights. From picturesque sunsets and boat excursions to cooking classes and exploring the Amalfi Coast, each day is crafted to create lasting memories with your loved one. Sorrento's charm, combined with its rich history and stunning landscapes, provides the ideal backdrop for a romantic getaway that you both will cherish forever. As you depart Sorrento, carry with you the warmth of its hospitality, the flavors of its cuisine, and the romance that lingers in the air.

Coastal itinerary

Embarking on a coastal itinerary in Sorrento is like stepping into a Mediterranean dream. Whether you're a history buff, a nature lover, or someone seeking culinary delights, Sorrento has something to offer for every traveler. we'll guide you through a mesmerizing journey along the Sorrentine Peninsula, exploring its stunning coastline and uncovering a myriad of activities.

Day 1: Arrival and Relaxation

Your coastal adventure begins with your arrival in Sorrento. Check into a charming hotel overlooking the sea to kickstart your experience with breathtaking views. After settling in, take a leisurely stroll along Marina Grande, a traditional fishing village. Enjoy a seafood dinner at one of the local restaurants, savoring the fresh catch of the day.

Day 2: Historical Exploration in Sorrento

Start your day with a visit to the historic center of Sorrento. Wander through the narrow streets lined with shops selling local crafts and delicacies. Don't miss the opportunity to taste limoncello, a traditional lemon liqueur produced in the region. Explore the impressive Cathedral of Sorrento and delve into the town's rich history at the Museo Correale di Terranova.

In the afternoon, take a short drive to the nearby archaeological site of Pompeii. Immerse yourself in the ancient ruins of this Roman city destroyed by the eruption of Mount Vesuvius in 79 AD. A guided tour will provide fascinating insights into daily life during the Roman Empire.

Day 3: Boat Excursion to Capri

Embark on a boat excursion to the glamorous island of Capri. The ferry ride itself offers stunning views of the Sorrentine coastline. Once on Capri, explore the famous Blue Grotto, a sea cave illuminated by a mesmerizing blue light. Visit the Gardens of Augustus for panoramic views of the Faraglioni rocks. Stroll through the charming streets of Capri Town and indulge in some shopping at high-end boutiques.

Return to Sorrento in the evening and unwind at a seaside restaurant, savoring a delicious dinner while watching the sunset over the Gulf of Naples.

Day 4: Hiking the Path of the Gods

For nature enthusiasts, today is dedicated to an invigorating hike along the Sentiero degli Dei, or the Path of the Gods. This trail offers breathtaking views of the Amalfi Coast and the Gulf of Salerno. The moderately challenging hike takes you through lush landscapes, past ancient stone houses, and along cliffside paths. Pack a picnic and take a break at one of the panoramic viewpoints.

After the hike, reward yourself with a relaxing evening at a local spa or a dip in the crystal-clear waters of the Mediterranean.

Day 5: Amalfi Coast Drive

Embark on one of the most iconic coastal drives in the world along the Amalfi Coast. Rent a convertible or hire a private driver for a leisurely journey through charming towns like Positano, Amalfi, and Ravello. Each stop offers unique attractions, from the colorful houses of Positano to the historic cathedral in Amalfi.

Enjoy a seafood lunch at a cliffside restaurant, and explore the gardens of Villa Rufolo in Ravello. End the day with a romantic dinner overlooking the twinkling lights of the Amalfi Coast.

Day 6: Cooking Class and Culinary Delights

Immerse yourself in the culinary delights of Sorrento with a hands-on cooking class. Learn to prepare traditional dishes such as pasta alle vongole and tiramisu. The class typically includes a visit to a local market to select fresh ingredients. Afterward, savor the fruits of your labor with a delicious lunch.

In the afternoon, explore the Sorrentine Peninsula's lesser-known gems, such as the charming village of Sant'Agata sui Due Golfi. Enjoy a leisurely evening, perhaps attending a local music or dance performance.

Day 7: Departure

On your final day, take some time to relax and reflect on the unforgettable experiences of your coastal itinerary in Sorrento. If time permits, revisit your favorite spots or explore any hidden gems you may have missed. Depart with cherished memories of the stunning landscapes, rich history, and warm hospitality that define this enchanting region.

This coastal itinerary in Sorrento promises a perfect blend of relaxation, exploration, and cultural immersion. Whether you're drawn to the historical sites, the natural beauty, or the culinary delights, Sorrento and its surrounding areas offer a truly magical experience along the Mediterranean coast.

Budget friendly itinerary

Creating a comprehensive budget-friendly itinerary for Sorrento with a plethora of activities is an exciting challenge. Let's dive into a detailed exploration of this charming destination.

Day 1: Arrival and Acquaintance

Morning

Arrive in Sorrento and check into your chosen budget-friendly accommodation.
Start your day with a traditional Italian breakfast at a local cafe. Enjoy a cappuccino and a pastry to kickstart your day.

Afternoon

Begin your exploration by strolling through the historic center of Sorrento. Admire the charming architecture and vibrant atmosphere.

Head to Piazza Tasso, the main square, and take in the lively ambiance. Consider grabbing a quick and affordable lunch at a nearby trattoria.

Evening

Dine at a local pizzeria for an authentic taste of Italy without breaking the bank.
Take a leisurely evening walk along the Marina Grande, enjoying the stunning sunset over the Bay of Naples.

Day 2: Historical Excursion

Morning

Visit the Museo Correale di Terranova, a budget-friendly museum showcasing the history and art of Sorrento.
Explore the town's historic churches, such as the Chiesa di San Francesco and the Basilica di Sant'Antonino.

Afternoon

Have a picnic in Villa Comunale, a beautiful public garden offering panoramic views of the Gulf of Naples.
Discover the charm of Sorrento's narrow streets and alleys, filled with local shops and artisanal products.

Evening

Enjoy dinner at a local osteria, where you can savor traditional Italian dishes at reasonable prices.

Day 3: Amalfi Coast Adventure

Morning

Take a budget-friendly ferry or bus to explore the Amalfi Coast. Visit Positano, known for its colorful houses and stunning cliffs.
Wander through the narrow streets and browse local boutiques for affordable souvenirs.

Afternoon

Continue your journey to Amalfi and visit the Duomo di Sant'Andrea, an impressive cathedral with a stunning facade. Have a budget-friendly seafood lunch at a local trattoria overlooking the sea.

Evening

Return to Sorrento and unwind at a cozy gelateria with a delicious gelato in hand.

Day 4: Cooking Class and Local Delicacies

Morning

Join a budget-friendly cooking class to learn the secrets of Italian cuisine. Enjoy the fruits of your labor for lunch.
Visit the local markets to purchase fresh ingredients for your cooking adventure.

Afternoon

Explore the backstreets of Sorrento, discovering hidden gems and capturing the essence of local life.

Try a panino or a slice of pizza from a street vendor for a quick and affordable snack.

Evening

Dine at a family-run trattoria, indulging in regional specialties without breaking the bank.

Day 5: Outdoor Escape

Morning

Embark on a budget-friendly hiking adventure along the Sorrento Peninsula. The Path of the Gods offers breathtaking views of the coastline.
Pack a picnic with local cheeses, olives, and fresh bread for a frugal yet delightful lunch.

Afternoon

Relax at one of Sorrento's free public beaches, such as Marina Grande or Puolo Beach.
Take a dip in the crystal-clear waters and soak up the Mediterranean sun.

Evening

Wrap up your outdoor day with a casual dinner at a local pizzeria or trattoria.

Day 6: Lemon Grove Exploration

Morning

Visit a local lemon grove to learn about the production of Limoncello, a famous Italian lemon liqueur.

Enjoy a budget-friendly breakfast with lemon-infused pastries and beverages.

Afternoon

Spend the afternoon at Vallone dei Mulini, a historic site with ruins of old mills surrounded by lush greenery.
Grab a slice of pizza or a sandwich from a local bakery for a cost-effective lunch.

Evening

Conclude your day with a sunset stroll along the cliffs of Sorrento, taking in the breathtaking views of the coastline.

Day 7: Departure

Morning

Before leaving, visit the Sorrento Cathedral and its serene cloister, a hidden gem in the heart of the town.
Enjoy a final Italian breakfast at your favorite local cafe.

Afternoon

Check out of your accommodation and bid farewell to Sorrento with a heart full of memories.

This budget-friendly itinerary in Sorrento provides a perfect balance of cultural exploration, outdoor adventures, and culinary delights without straining your wallet. Enjoy your journey in this picturesque Italian paradise!

Historical itinerary
Embark on a journey through the enchanting streets of Sorrento, where history comes alive, and every cobblestone

whispers tales of the past. This historical itinerary is designed to immerse you in the rich tapestry of Sorrento's past while offering a plethora of activities to make your visit truly unforgettable.

Day 1: Exploring the Old Town
Morning:

Start your historical adventure by strolling through the heart of Sorrento—the Old Town. Begin at Piazza Tasso, named after the renowned poet Torquato Tasso, and marvel at the lively atmosphere of this central square. Admire the Baroque beauty of the Church of Carmine, a hidden gem that houses remarkable artworks.

Afternoon:

Lunch at a traditional trattoria, where you can savor authentic Sorrentine dishes. As you dine, learn about the town's maritime history at the Museo della Tarsia Lignea, featuring intricate wood inlays from Sorrento's boat-building heritage.

Evening:

Take a leisurely walk to the Vallone dei Mulini, an abandoned mill valley, and imagine the bustling activity that once filled this industrial hub. End your day with a relaxing dinner at a seaside restaurant, savoring local seafood and panoramic views.

Day 2: Sorrento's Ancient Roots
Morning:

Visit the Archaeological Museum of Sorrento to discover artifacts from the ancient Roman town of Sorrentum. Marvel at well-preserved frescoes, sculptures, and everyday items that provide insight into daily life during the Roman era.

Afternoon:

Explore the Villa Pollio Felice, a Roman villa with breathtaking views of the Gulf of Naples. Wander through the well-preserved rooms and gardens, where the echoes of the past are still palpable.

Evening:

Dine at a traditional osteria, enjoying local specialties. Afterward, attend a performance at the Teatro Tasso, a historic theater that has entertained audiences for centuries.

Day 3: A Taste of Sorrentine Art
Morning:

Begin your day at the Correale di Terranova Museum, home to an impressive collection of decorative arts and artifacts. Admire the exquisite porcelain and majolica pieces that showcase Sorrento's artistic heritage.

Afternoon:

Participate in a hands-on workshop to learn the art of intarsia, a traditional Sorrentine wood inlay technique. Create your own masterpiece under the guidance of skilled artisans, connecting with the town's artistic roots.

Evening:

Dine in the charming Marina Grande, a historic fishing village with colorful houses and waterfront restaurants.

Enjoy fresh catch-of-the-day dishes and soak in the romantic ambiance.

Day 4: Coastal Beauty and Ancient Ruins

Morning:

Embark on a boat tour along the Amalfi Coast, taking in the breathtaking scenery of cliffs, coves, and crystal-clear waters. Visit the ancient Roman villa, Villa di Pollio, nestled on the coastline, and explore its ruins.

Afternoon:

Indulge in a leisurely lunch at a seaside trattoria, savoring the flavors of the Mediterranean. Take a stroll through the lemon groves, learning about Sorrento's famed limoncello production.

Evening:

Cap off your historical journey with a sunset visit to the Punta del Capo, where the ruins of a Roman villa overlook the sea. Enjoy the spectacular view as the sun sets on Sorrento, casting a golden glow on its timeless beauty.

Practical Tips:

- Local Cuisine: Don't miss out on trying Sorrento's specialties, including gnocchi alla sorrentina, seafood risotto, and, of course, the famous limoncello.

- Guided Tours: Consider joining guided tours for in-depth insights into Sorrento's history and culture. Local guides often share fascinating stories that you might miss otherwise.

- Comfortable Footwear: Sorrento's streets can be cobblestone-paved and hilly. Ensure you have comfortable footwear for exploring the town and its historical sites.

- Seasonal Considerations: Sorrento is beautiful year-round, but the summer months can be crowded. Consider visiting during the shoulder seasons for a more relaxed experience.

This historical itinerary in Sorrento promises a perfect blend of cultural immersion and leisure, offering a deep dive into the town's captivating past while creating lasting memories of its timeless charm. Whether you're a history enthusiast, an art lover, or simply seeking a picturesque getaway, Sorrento's historical treasures await your exploration.

Family friendly itinerary

Here's a family-friendly itinerary for your Sorrento trip, packed with activities to keep everyone entertained:

Day 1: Arrival and Get Acquainted with Sorrento

Morning:
Arrive in Sorrento and settle into your accommodation. Choose a family-friendly hotel or vacation rental that suits your needs.

Afternoon:
Take a leisurely stroll through Sorrento's historic center. Visit Piazza Tasso, the main square, and let the kids enjoy some gelato from one of the local shops. Explore the narrow streets lined with shops selling local crafts and souvenirs.

Evening:
Dine at a family-friendly restaurant. Sorrento offers a variety of options, from traditional Italian to international cuisine. Relax and enjoy your first evening in this charming town.

Day 2: Explore the Amalfi Coast

Morning:
Take a day trip to the Amalfi Coast. Consider a boat tour to explore the picturesque coastline. Visit Positano, Amalfi, and Ravello. Each town has its own unique charm and plenty of opportunities for family-friendly activities.

Afternoon:
Have a picnic on the beach or enjoy lunch at a seaside restaurant. Let the kids play in the sand while you soak in the stunning views of the Mediterranean.

Evening:
Return to Sorrento in the evening and have a quiet dinner at a local restaurant. Reflect on the beauty of the Amalfi Coast with your family.

Day 3: Historical Exploration

Morning:
Visit the archaeological site of Pompeii. It's an educational and fascinating experience for both adults and kids. Consider hiring a guide who can make the history come alive for your family.

Afternoon:
Have lunch in Pompeii or return to Sorrento for a relaxing afternoon. Consider exploring the Museo Correale di Terranova, which houses a diverse collection of art and artifacts.

Evening:
Choose a restaurant with a view for dinner. Many restaurants in Sorrento offer panoramic views of the Gulf of Naples, creating a memorable dining experience.

Day 4: Cooking Class and Lemon Grove Visit

Morning:
Take a family-friendly cooking class to learn how to make traditional Italian dishes. It's a hands-on experience that both kids and adults can enjoy.

Afternoon:
Visit a local lemon grove. Sorrento is famous for its lemons, and a guided tour of a lemon farm can be both educational and entertaining for the whole family.

Evening:
Prepare a dinner with the recipes you learned in the cooking class using fresh local ingredients. Enjoy a homemade meal as a family.

Day 5: Beach Day and Water Activities

Morning:
Spend the morning at one of Sorrento's beautiful beaches. Relax on the sand while the kids play in the shallow waters.

Afternoon:
Engage in water activities like paddleboarding or kayaking. Many beaches offer equipment rentals for a fun-filled afternoon.

Evening:
Dine at a beachfront restaurant for a sunset dinner. Enjoy the sea breeze and the sound of the waves as you wrap up your day.

Day 6: Hiking in the Hills

Morning:
Embark on a family-friendly hike in the hills surrounding Sorrento. The trails offer stunning views of the coastline and the Bay of Naples.

Afternoon:
Have a picnic at a scenic spot along the hiking trail. Let the kids explore nature and enjoy the outdoors.

Evening:
Return to Sorrento and treat yourselves to a well-deserved dinner at a local trattoria. Share stories of your day and appreciate the beauty of Sorrento's landscapes.

Day 7: Relaxation and Departure

Morning:
Spend your last morning in Sorrento at a local spa or wellness center. Relax and unwind before heading home.

Afternoon:
Have a farewell lunch at a favorite restaurant or try a new spot you haven't visited yet.

Evening:
Depart from Sorrento, cherishing the memories you've created with your family in this enchanting Italian destination.

This itinerary offers a mix of cultural exploration, outdoor activities, and relaxation, ensuring a memorable and enjoyable family vacation in Sorrento.

Chapter 5: Cultural Experiences

Festival and Events

Sorrento is not only known for its stunning views of the Bay of Naples but also for its vibrant and lively festivals and events throughout the year. These celebrations bring together locals and tourists alike, creating a festive atmosphere that showcases the rich cultural heritage of this charming destination.

One of the most anticipated events in Sorrento is the Settembrata Anacaprese, a month-long celebration held in September. This festival is dedicated to the island of Capri, located just a short boat ride away from Sorrento. During Settembrata Anacaprese, the streets come alive with colorful decorations, traditional music, and lively dance performances. Local artisans showcase their crafts, offering visitors a chance to purchase unique handmade souvenirs. The highlight of the festival is the food, with numerous stalls offering delicious Caprese dishes and local specialties.

Sorrento also hosts the annual Lemon Festival, known as "Sagra del Limone." This event takes place in the spring when the lemon groves are in full bloom. The town's streets are adorned with lemon-themed decorations, creating a vibrant and citrusy atmosphere. Visitors can enjoy parades, live music, and dance performances, all celebrating the beloved lemon. Local restaurants and vendors offer a variety of lemon-infused dishes, from refreshing lemonade to zesty lemon desserts.

For those who appreciate the arts, the Sorrento Film Festival is a must-attend event. Held annually, this festival showcases a diverse selection of national and international films, attracting filmmakers, actors, and film enthusiasts from around the world. The picturesque backdrop of Sorrento adds a touch of magic to the cinematic experience. Q&A sessions with filmmakers and actors, as well as workshops and panel discussions, provide an opportunity for attendees to engage with the creative minds behind the films.

In the summer, the Estate Musicale Chigiana brings classical music to Sorrento. This music festival, organized by the Chigiana Academy of Siena, features performances by talented musicians and orchestras. Concerts take place in various historic venues, including the Cloister of San Francesco and the Sedile Dominova, providing a unique and enchanting setting for classical music enthusiasts.

The religious festival of Saint Anne, the patron saint of Sorrento, is celebrated with great fervor and devotion. The Feast of Saint Anne, known as the Festa di Sant'Anna, takes place in July and includes religious processions, solemn Masses, and vibrant celebrations throughout the town. Locals and visitors come together to honor Saint Anne, creating a sense of unity and community spirit.

Sorrento's love for seafood is showcased in the Settembre di Gusta, a month-long celebration of the region's culinary delights. September is a prime time for seafood, and local restaurants participate by offering special menus featuring the freshest catches of the season. From succulent seafood pastas to grilled fish, Settembre di Gusta is a paradise for food lovers.

The Tarantella Festival is a lively and energetic event that celebrates the traditional dance of the same name. This folk dance, characterized by fast and rhythmic movements, is an integral part of Southern Italian culture. During the festival, the streets of Sorrento come alive with dancers clad in colorful traditional costumes, moving to the beat of the tambourines and mandolins. Visitors can join in the fun by learning the basic steps of the Tarantella or simply enjoy the captivating performances.

Sorrento's Carnival is another highlight, bringing a burst of color and excitement to the town. The streets are filled with elaborate costumes, vibrant masks, and lively music during the Carnival season. Parades featuring floats, dancers, and performers entertain the crowds, creating a festive and joyous atmosphere. Local businesses often participate in the festivities, decorating their storefronts and offering special promotions to enhance the Carnival spirit.

Throughout the year, Sorrento also hosts a variety of cultural events, art exhibitions, and food and wine tastings. These smaller-scale gatherings provide a more intimate experience for visitors looking to explore the local arts and flavors. The Correale Museum of Terracotta, located in a historic building, regularly hosts exhibitions showcasing the work of local and international artists.

In addition to these recurring events, Sorrento occasionally hosts special celebrations and festivals to mark significant occasions. Whether it's a historical anniversary, a cultural milestone, or a seasonal celebration, Sorrento takes pride in creating memorable and enjoyable experiences for everyone.

For those planning a visit to Sorrento, it's advisable to check the event calendar in advance to align their trip with the festivals and events that interest them the most. Whether you're a music enthusiast, a foodie, or a culture lover, Sorrento's diverse and lively calendar of events ensures there's always something exciting happening in this charming coastal town.

Historical Sites and Museums

Here, we'll delve into the historical sites and museums that make Sorrento a treasure trove for history enthusiasts.

1. Seductive Sirens and Ancient Legends: The Land of Sorrento

Sorrento's allure is deeply rooted in ancient myths, particularly the tale of Odysseus and the sirens. The Li Galli islands, just off the coast, are believed to be the home of these mesmerizing creatures. While the exact location of the sirens' enchanting song may remain a mystery, the breathtaking views from Sorrento's cliffs offer a glimpse into the mythical landscapes that inspired such legends. Visitors can take boat tours from the Marina Grande to explore these legendary waters and contemplate the captivating stories that have echoed through the ages.

2. The Charming Piazza Tasso: Heart of Sorrento

Piazza Tasso serves as the pulsating heart of Sorrento, named after the renowned 16th-century poet Torquato Tasso. Located in the historic center, the square is surrounded by historic buildings, lively cafes, and charming shops. Notable landmarks include the Baroque Church of Carmine and the Palazzo Correale, each contributing to the square's rich historical tapestry. Piazza Tasso is easily accessible and serves as an excellent starting point for exploring the city's historical gems.

3. Sorrento Cathedral: A Testament to Faith

The Sorrento Cathedral, dedicated to Saints Philip and James, stands proudly on the Corso Italia. Its impressive facade, featuring intricate detailing and a stunning rose window, beckons visitors to explore its sacred interior. The address, Piazza della Santissima Annunziata, leads you to this architectural marvel where you can marvel at the centuries-old artwork and feel the spiritual resonance that permeates the air. The cathedral is not only a religious landmark but also a repository of Sorrento's spiritual history.

4. Museo Correale di Terranova: Art and History Unveiled

Located on Via Correale, the Museo Correale di Terranova is housed in a neoclassical villa with panoramic views of the Gulf of Naples. The museum's address, Via Correale, 50, Sorrento, invites visitors to embark on a journey through Sorrento's artistic evolution. The extensive collection includes paintings by prominent artists, decorative arts, and precious porcelain. The villa itself is a work of art, adding to the immersive experience of exploring Sorrento's cultural heritage.

5. The Ancient Walls of Sorrento: Guardians of Time

The ancient walls of Sorrento, dating back to the 6th century, encircle the historic center. The primary entrance, Porta Parsano, provides access to the charming streets within. Addressed at Via S. Francesco, these walls offer panoramic views of the Gulf of Naples and the surrounding landscape. Each stone of the fortifications whispers tales of invasions, battles, and the resilience of Sorrento throughout history. Taking a leisurely walk along these walls allows visitors to appreciate the strategic importance of this defensive structure.

6. Baths of Queen Giovanna: An Oasis of Tranquility

Nestled between Punta del Capo and the Bay of Ieranto, the Baths of Queen Giovanna are accessible from Via Capo. Follow the trail to this hidden gem and discover the ruins of an ancient Roman villa overlooking the Tyrrhenian Sea. The address, Via Capo, 30, Sorrento, guides you to this serene retreat. Queen Giovanna's Baths offer a unique blend of history and natural beauty, providing a peaceful escape where visitors can immerse themselves in the crystal-clear waters while surrounded by the echoes of royalty.

7. Chiostro di San Francesco: A Cloister of Serenity

Venture to the Chiostro di San Francesco, adjacent to the Church of San Francesco on Via San Francesco. This tranquil cloister, dating back to the 14th century, is a hidden sanctuary away from the bustling streets. The address, Via San Francesco, 1, Sorrento, leads you to this serene haven. Admire the elegant columns and verdant garden, where time seems to stand still. The cloister provides a glimpse into the daily lives of Franciscan friars and offers a peaceful retreat for contemplation.

8. Deep Dive into Archaeological Treasures: Museo Archeologico George Vallet

Situated at Via della Pietà, 52, Sorrento, the Museo Archeologico George Vallet is a treasure trove of archaeological wonders. The museum's diverse collection spans prehistoric to Roman times, with artifacts that unveil Sorrento's rich past. From ancient tools to intricate pottery, each exhibit narrates a chapter of the region's history. The address beckons history enthusiasts to embark on a captivating journey through time, exploring the cultural heritage that defines Sorrento.

9. Vallone dei Mulini: Industrial Remnants in Nature's Embrace

Discover Vallone dei Mulini, or the Valley of the Mills, by following Via Fuorimura. This hidden valley, surrounded by lush vegetation, is home to abandoned 19th-century flour mills. The address, Via Fuorimura, Sorrento, leads you to this enchanting site where industrial remnants harmonize with the beauty of nature. Imagine the once-bustling activity as you stroll through this picturesque landscape, where the echoes of the mills blend seamlessly with the rustling leaves and flowing water.

10. The Marina Grande: Fishing Traditions and Seaside Charm

Conclude your historical exploration at the Marina Grande, easily accessible from the city center. The picturesque fishing village, with its colorful buildings and vibrant waterfront, preserves the city's maritime traditions. The address, Marina Grande, Sorrento, guides you to this authentic enclave where fishermen mend nets and boats bob in the azure waters. Indulge in fresh seafood at one of the waterfront restaurants, savoring the flavors of Sorrento's maritime history against the backdrop of the Tyrrhenian Sea.

In conclusion, Sorrento's historical sites and museums weave a captivating tapestry that spans millennia. From ancient legends to medieval walls and archaeological wonders, each site tells a story of Sorrento's evolution through time. Whether you're a history enthusiast or a casual traveler, Sorrento's rich heritage is sure to leave an indelible impression, inviting you to immerse yourself in the magic of this coastal gem.

Chapter 6: Off the Beaten Path Adventures

Hidden Gems & lesser known Destinations to check out

While popular attractions like the Amalfi Coast and the historic town center are must-see destinations, there are hidden gems and lesser-known spots that promise unique and memorable experiences. In this guide, we'll uncover some of Sorrento's best-kept secrets, complete with their addresses to ensure you can explore them on your next visit.

1. Villa Pollio

Nestled along the scenic Via Nastro Verde, Villa Pollio stands as a testament to Sorrento's rich history. This hidden gem is a private villa that opens its gates to visitors seeking a serene escape. The well-manicured gardens boast vibrant flora, and the ancient ruins within the estate offer a glimpse into the region's past. Overlooking the Gulf of Naples, the villa provides a breathtaking backdrop for leisurely strolls and peaceful contemplation. The address for this enchanting retreat is Via Nastro Verde, 1, 80067 Sorrento NA, Italy.

2. Marina di Puolo

Escape the tourist traps and discover the authenticity of Marina di Puolo. Located in Massa Lubrense, this hidden coastal haven is characterized by its charming fishing village atmosphere. Colorful boats bob in the crystal-clear waters, creating a picturesque scene that captures the essence of local life. The seafood restaurants that line the shore offer a taste of the region's culinary delights. To experience the charm of Marina di Puolo, head to Marina di Puolo, 80061 Massa Lubrense NA, Italy.

3. Valle dei Mulini

For a journey back in time, explore the historic Valle dei Mulini, or Valley of Mills. Located on Via Fuorimura, this hidden valley reveals the remnants of ancient mills that once powered Sorrento's thriving pasta industry. The overgrown ruins add a mystical touch to the landscape, making it a haven for history enthusiasts and photographers alike. The address for this intriguing site is Via Fuorimura, 80067 Sorrento NA, Italy.

4. Bagni della Regina Giovanna

Tucked away along Via Capo, Bagni della Regina Giovanna offers a secluded escape with a touch of royal history. Legend has it that this hidden cove was a favorite bathing spot for Queen Joanna II of Naples. The natural pool, formed by the surrounding rocks, adds a touch of magic to this hidden paradise. To bask in the beauty of Bagni della Regina Giovanna, head to Via Capo, 80067 Sorrento NA, Italy.

5. Museo Correale di Terranova

While not entirely off the beaten path, Museo Correale di Terranova often goes unnoticed amid Sorrento's more famous attractions. Located on Via Correale, this museum houses a remarkable collection of Neapolitan paintings, decorative arts, and rare artifacts. Take a leisurely stroll through its elegant halls to immerse yourself in the cultural heritage of the region. The museum's address is Via Correale, 50, 80067 Sorrento NA, Italy.

6. Vallone dei Mulini

Distinct from Valle dei Mulini, Vallone dei Mulini is another hidden valley awaiting discovery. Located on Via Fuorimura, this lush green paradise offers meandering paths and the remains of ancient mills, creating a serene environment away from the bustling crowds. The address for this lesser-known retreat is Via Fuorimura, 80067 Sorrento NA, Italy.

7. Antico Borgo Marinaro

Step back in time and explore the charming streets of Antico Borgo Marinaro, the Old Fishermen's Village. Situated on Via Marina Grande, this neighborhood is a tapestry of narrow alleyways, colorful buildings, and a laid-back ambiance. It's the perfect place for a leisurely stroll, allowing you to discover local shops and traditional trattorias. The address for this quaint village is Via Marina Grande, 80067 Sorrento NA, Italy.

8. Punta Campanella

Nature enthusiasts will find paradise at Punta Campanella, a scenic headland offering panoramic views of the Gulf of Naples and the Amalfi Coast. Located on Via Nastro Azzurro in Massa Lubrense, this protected nature reserve is a haven for hikers. Trails lead to hidden coves, ancient watchtowers, and vistas that will leave you in awe of Sorrento's natural beauty.

9. Chiostro di San Francesco

Amidst the historic center, discover the hidden gem of Chiostro di San Francesco. Located on Via San Francesco, this cloister offers a peaceful retreat with a tranquil garden. Ancient columns, fragrant flowers, and a sense of serenity make it an ideal spot for a quiet moment of reflection. The address for this hidden oasis is Via San Francesco, 1, 80067 Sorrento NA, Italy.

10. Il Vallone dei Mulini

For a unique perspective of Sorrento, head to Il Vallone dei Mulini. Located on Via Fuorimura, this lesser-known viewpoint provides a breathtaking panorama of Sorrento's rooftops and the surrounding landscape. Capture the beauty of the town from a different angle, away from the crowds that usually flock to the more popular viewpoints. The address for this scenic spot is Via Fuorimura, 80067 Sorrento NA, Italy.

Exploring these hidden gems and lesser-known destinations in Sorrento will add a touch of mystery and discovery to your Italian adventure. Whether you're seeking historical sites, natural beauty, or a quiet escape, these off-the-beaten-path locations will ensure a memorable and authentic experience in this enchanting coastal town.

Fun things to do during your visit

Whether you're a history buff, a foodie, or just looking for a relaxing getaway, Sorrento has something to offer for everyone. Here's a guide to fun things to do during your visit to Sorrento, ensuring you make the most of your time in this picturesque destination.

Explore the Historic Old Town

Sorrento's Old Town is a labyrinth of narrow streets, charming alleyways, and historical buildings that date back centuries. Take a leisurely stroll through the cobblestone streets, and you'll discover quaint shops, local markets, and traditional Italian architecture. Don't forget to visit the Piazza Tasso, the main square, where you can sip on a cappuccino at one of the outdoor cafes and soak in the lively atmosphere.

Visit the Duomo

The Sorrento Cathedral, or Duomo, is a must-visit for history enthusiasts. Built in the 15th century, the cathedral boasts a stunning facade and houses beautiful frescoes and artworks. The highlight, however, is the impressive bell tower, offering panoramic views of Sorrento and the Bay of Naples. It's a climb to the top, but the breathtaking scenery makes it well worth the effort.

Indulge in Local Cuisine

Sorrento is famous for its delectable cuisine, and no visit is complete without savoring the local dishes. Try the fresh seafood at a seaside restaurant, indulge in a plate of homemade pasta, and don't forget to sample the region's renowned lemon-based dishes. Limoncello, a lemon-flavored liqueur, is a popular after-dinner drink and makes for a great souvenir to take home.

Take a Boat Tour to Capri

Sorrento is a gateway to the beautiful island of Capri, just a short boat ride away. Arrange a boat tour and explore the crystal-clear waters surrounding the island. Visit the Blue Grotto, a sea cave illuminated by a unique blue light, and take in the stunning landscapes. Capri is also known for its upscale shopping and charming cafes, providing a perfect day excursion from Sorrento.

Hike the Path of the Gods

For nature enthusiasts, the Path of the Gods (Sentiero degli Dei) is a hiking trail that offers breathtaking views of the Amalfi Coast. The trail takes you through picturesque landscapes, ancient villages, and rugged terrain. Be sure to wear comfortable shoes, carry water, and take your time to appreciate the natural beauty along the way.

Relax on Sorrento's Beaches

Sorrento may not be known for its expansive sandy beaches, but it offers several small coves and rocky shores perfect for a relaxing day by the sea. Marina Grande and Marina Piccola are two popular spots where you can soak up the sun, swim in the clear waters, and enjoy a gelato from one of the local vendors.

Discover the Ancient Ruins of Pompeii

A short drive from Sorrento, the ancient city of Pompeii is a UNESCO World Heritage site and a fascinating archaeological wonder. Buried by the eruption of Mount Vesuvius in 79 AD, Pompeii provides a glimpse into daily life during the Roman Empire. Wander through well-preserved streets, marvel at ancient frescoes, and imagine the city as it once was.

Attend a Musical Performance

Sorrento has a vibrant cultural scene, and you might be fortunate enough to catch a live musical performance during your visit. Check local event listings for concerts, operas, or traditional Italian music performances. The combination of music, charming venues, and the warm Mediterranean breeze creates a memorable experience.

Visit the Museo Correale di Terranova

Art and history enthusiasts will appreciate a visit to the Museo Correale di Terranova. This museum houses an impressive collection of art, furniture, and decorative items from the 17th to the 19th centuries. The museum is set in a beautiful villa with lush gardens, providing a peaceful escape from the bustling streets of Sorrento.

Explore the Amalfi Coast

Sorrento serves as an ideal starting point for exploring the stunning Amalfi Coast. Rent a car or take a scenic bus ride along the coastline, and you'll encounter charming villages like Positano, Amalfi, and Ravello. Each village has its own unique character, with colorful buildings, historic churches, and breathtaking views of the Mediterranean.

Attend a Cooking Class

Immerse yourself in the local culture by taking a cooking class to learn the secrets of traditional Italian cuisine. Local chefs will guide you through the preparation of authentic dishes, from handmade pasta to classic desserts. It's a hands-on experience that not only results in a delicious meal but also provides you with skills to recreate the flavors of Sorrento back home.

Enjoy Sunset at Villa Comunale

Villa Comunale is a beautiful public park with well-manicured gardens and stunning views of the Gulf of Naples. Take a leisurely stroll through the park, find a comfortable spot, and witness a breathtaking sunset over the

Mediterranean. It's a romantic and peaceful way to end your day in Sorrento.

Take a Day Trip to Naples

If you have extra time, consider taking a day trip to Naples, a city rich in history, art, and vibrant street life. Explore the historic center, visit the Naples National Archaeological Museum, and, of course, indulge in authentic Neapolitan pizza. Naples is easily accessible by train or car from Sorrento.

Learn about Traditional Crafts

Sorrento has a long tradition of craftsmanship, especially in the art of inlaid woodwork. Visit one of the local workshops to witness artisans creating intricate designs using different types of wood. You can purchase unique souvenirs, from small trinkets to larger furniture pieces, to commemorate your visit.

Attend a Wine Tasting

Southern Italy is renowned for its wine, and Sorrento offers the perfect opportunity to sample local varieties. Attend a wine tasting session where you can try regional wines paired with delicious Italian cheeses and cured meats. Learn about the winemaking process and discover your new favorite vintage.

Participate in a Festivity

Check the local calendar for festivals and events happening during your visit. Sorrento hosts various celebrations throughout the year, ranging from religious processions to music festivals. Participating in a local festivity allows you to experience the vibrant culture and traditions of the region.

Engage in Water Activities

For those seeking more active pursuits, Sorrento offers a range of water activities. Rent a kayak and explore the coastline from a different perspective, or try your hand at paddleboarding for a fun and refreshing experience. Many local providers offer equipment rental and guided tours for water enthusiasts of all skill levels.

Visit the Valley of the Mills

The Valley of the Mills (Valle dei Mulini) is a unique and historic site in Sorrento. It's a deep ravine where several old mills once operated, powered by the water from a nearby stream. Although the mills are no longer in use, the valley provides a picturesque setting for a leisurely walk and a glimpse into Sorrento's industrial past.

Take a Lemon Tour

Sorrento is famous for its lemons, and you can't leave without learning about the cultivation and production of these iconic fruits. Join a lemon tour to visit local orchards, learn about the traditional cultivation methods, and, of course, taste some freshly squeezed lemonade or limoncello.

Explore the Chiostro di San Francesco

The Chiostro di San Francesco is a hidden gem in Sorrento, often overlooked by tourists. This tranquil cloister dates back to the 14th century and features a beautiful garden surrounded by arched porticos. It's a serene spot to escape the hustle and bustle of the town and appreciate the historical and architectural beauty of Sorrento.

Attend a Puppet Show

For a unique and entertaining experience, catch a traditional puppet show in Sorrento. Puppetry has a long history in Italian culture, and you can witness skillful puppeteers performing traditional stories with intricately crafted puppets. It's a delightful cultural experience for visitors of all ages.

Take a Scenic Train Ride

Embark on a scenic train ride along the Circumvesuviana Railway, connecting Sorrento to Naples. The journey offers breathtaking views of the Bay of Naples and Mount Vesuvius. Sit back, relax, and enjoy the picturesque landscapes as the train winds its way through charming towns and coastal scenery.

Visit the Basilica di Sant'Antonino

The Basilica di Sant'Antonino is a religious landmark in Sorrento dedicated to the town's patron saint. Admire the impressive architecture, including the Baroque facade and the beautiful interior adorned with frescoes. The basilica is a peaceful retreat, and its elevated position provides panoramic views of Sorrento and the surrounding areas.

Attend a Cultural Event at Tasso Theatre

Check the schedule at Tasso Theatre for cultural events, including live performances, concerts, and theatrical productions. This historic theater, located in the heart of Sorrento, provides a charming venue to experience the local arts scene. Enjoy a night of entertainment and immerse yourself in the cultural offerings of the town.

Take a Dip in the Baths of Queen Giovanna

For a unique beach experience, visit the Baths of Queen Giovanna. This historic site features natural pools and ruins along the coast, offering a secluded spot to swim and relax. The crystal-clear waters and historical ambiance make it a hidden gem for those looking to escape the more crowded beaches.

Explore the Sorrento Coastline by Bike

Rent a bike and explore the stunning Sorrento coastline at your own pace. Follow the coastal roads, enjoy the sea breeze, and stop at scenic viewpoints along the way. Cycling is a fantastic way to appreciate the natural beauty of the area while staying active during your visit.

Attend a Language or Cooking Workshop

Immerse yourself in the local culture by participating in a language or cooking workshop. Engage with locals, learn basic Italian phrases, and gain insights into the art of Italian cuisine. These interactive experiences not only enhance your travel experience but also provide a deeper connection to the community.

Capture Memories with a Photography Tour

Sorrento's picturesque landscapes and charming streets offer countless opportunities for stunning photographs. Consider joining a photography tour to discover the best vantage points, learn new techniques, and capture memorable moments of your visit. Whether you're a seasoned photographer or a beginner, you'll appreciate the beauty that Sorrento has to offer.

Join a Yoga or Wellness Retreat

Escape the hustle of daily life by joining a yoga or wellness retreat in Sorrento. Many hotels and retreat centers offer programs that include yoga sessions, meditation, and holistic wellness activities. It's a rejuvenating way to balance your exploration of the town with moments of relaxation and self-care.

Discover Local Art Galleries

Sorrento is home to several art galleries showcasing the works of local and international artists. Explore these galleries to discover paintings, sculptures, and contemporary art that reflects the cultural richness of the region. You may even find a unique piece of art to bring home as a special souvenir.

Attend a Religious Procession

If your visit coincides with a religious festival or celebration, consider attending a traditional procession. These events often include colorful parades, music, and a vibrant display of local culture. It's a unique opportunity to witness the religious traditions that are an integral part of Sorrento's identity.

Sample Gelato at Puro e Bio

Indulge your sweet tooth with a visit to Puro e Bio, a popular gelateria in Sorrento known for its organic and natural gelato. Choose from a variety of flavors made with high-quality ingredients, and savor the creamy goodness as you stroll through the charming streets of the town.

Chapter 7: Practical Information

Safety and Security Considerations

While Sorrento is a relatively safe destination, like any other place, it's essential to be mindful of safety and security considerations to ensure a smooth and enjoyable visit. This comprehensive guide will walk you through various aspects of safety, from general travel tips to specific precautions for different situations.

1. General Travel Tips

a. Research and Planning

Before embarking on your journey to Sorrento, conduct thorough research about the destination. Familiarize yourself with the local customs, emergency contacts, and any travel advisories that may be in place. Ensure your accommodations are in a safe neighborhood and have positive reviews regarding security.

b. Stay Informed

Keep abreast of current events in Sorrento and Italy in general. Sign up for travel alerts and notifications to stay informed about any potential risks or developments that may affect your visit.

c. Secure Your Belongings

Tourist destinations often attract petty criminals. Be vigilant and keep your belongings secure. Use anti-theft bags, and avoid displaying valuable items in public. Consider purchasing travel insurance to safeguard against potential losses.

2. Transportation Safety

a. Public Transportation

Sorrento has a well-connected public transportation system, including buses and ferries. While generally safe, be cautious of pickpockets, especially in crowded areas. Keep an eye on your belongings and be aware of your surroundings.

b. Driving

If you plan to rent a car, familiarize yourself with local traffic rules. Italian roads can be narrow and winding, so drive cautiously. Park in well-lit and designated areas, and never leave valuables in your vehicle.

c. Walking

Sorrento's charming streets are best explored on foot. Stick to well-lit paths, especially at night. Avoid poorly lit or isolated areas, and be cautious when crossing streets.

3. Accommodation Safety

a. Choose Reputable Accommodations

Opt for reputable hotels and guesthouses with positive reviews regarding safety. Ensure that the accommodation has secure access, well-lit common areas, and a reliable security system.

b. Room Safety

Use the hotel safe to store valuables such as passports, extra cash, and electronic devices. Keep your room secure by using all available locks and deadbolts when inside.

4. Health and Medical Considerations

a. Travel Insurance

Ensure you have comprehensive travel insurance that covers medical emergencies. Familiarize yourself with the local healthcare facilities and their contact information.

b. Medications and Vaccinations

Check if any vaccinations are required before traveling to Sorrento. Bring an ample supply of any necessary medications and carry a basic first aid kit.

c. Drinking Water

While tap water in Sorrento is generally safe to drink, some may prefer bottled water. Stay hydrated, especially during the warmer months.

5. Emergency Preparedness

a. Emergency Contacts

Save local emergency contacts, including the nearest embassy or consulate, in your phone. It's also advisable to have a list of important contacts in both digital and physical formats.

b. Know Your Location

Familiarize yourself with the location of the nearest hospitals, police stations, and emergency exits in public spaces.

6. Cultural Sensitivity

a. Respect Local Customs

Respect the local culture and customs of Sorrento. Dress modestly when visiting religious sites, and be mindful of local traditions.

b. Language

While English is widely spoken, learning a few basic Italian phrases can go a long way in enhancing your experience and building positive connections with locals.

7. Socializing Safely

a. Nightlife

Enjoying Sorrento's nightlife is a must, but exercise caution. Stay in well-lit areas, travel in groups, and avoid excessive alcohol consumption.

b. Social Media Awareness

Be mindful of what you share on social media. Avoid posting your exact location in real-time, especially when you're away from your accommodation.

Conclusion

Sorrento offers a magical experience for travelers, and with proper precautions, you can ensure a safe and enjoyable visit. By staying informed, being vigilant, and respecting local customs, you can make the most of your time in this enchanting destination. Safe travels!

Transportation & Getting around

Navigating this picturesque town and its surroundings becomes a key aspect of ensuring a seamless and enjoyable visit. In this guide, we'll explore the various transportation options available and provide tips on getting around Sorrento and its neighboring gems.

1. Arrival in Sorrento

a. By Air

If you're arriving by air, your gateway to Sorrento is Naples International Airport, the closest major airport to this charming town. Once you've landed, a range of transportation options awaits to seamlessly whisk you away to your destination on the Amalfi Coast.

Shuttle Services:
One of the most convenient and hassle-free options is opting for shuttle services. These dedicated services operate regular routes between Naples Airport and Sorrento, providing a comfortable and scenic journey. The shuttles are often equipped with amenities to make your ride enjoyable, allowing you to relax and take in the breathtaking views as you approach your destination.

Taxi:
For those seeking a more personalized and flexible mode of transportation, taxis are readily available at the airport. While this option offers the freedom to travel at your own pace, it's crucial to establish the fare with the driver before embarking on your journey. This ensures transparency and avoids any surprises at the end of your ride.

Public Transportation:
If you're inclined towards a budget-friendly option, public transportation is a viable choice. The Circumvesuviana train, connecting Naples to Sorrento, is a popular and economical way to travel. The train journey not only offers a cost-effective solution but also allows you to witness the Italian countryside during your transit.

b. By Sea

Sorrento's coastal location provides a captivating entry point for those arriving by sea. If your journey involves island hopping or a scenic coastal route, ferries and hydrofoils become not just a means of transportation but an integral part of your Sorrento experience.

i. Ferries

Ferries offer a leisurely and scenic way to approach Sorrento. From the deck, you'll be treated to breathtaking views of the Gulf of Naples and the rugged coastline. Several ferry companies operate routes connecting Sorrento to neighboring islands such as Capri, Ischia, and Procida. The leisurely pace of the ferry ride allows you to soak in the beauty of the Tyrrhenian Sea.

ii. Hydrofoils

For those seeking a quicker transit, hydrofoils are a popular choice. These high-speed vessels provide a faster connection between Sorrento and nearby coastal towns and islands. With their hydrofoil technology, these boats glide over the water, ensuring a swift and efficient journey.
iii. Marina Piccola and Marina Grande

Upon arriving by sea, you'll find yourself greeted by Sorrento's two main ports—Marina Piccola and Marina Grande. Each has its unique charm and serves as a gateway to different facets of Sorrento.

- Marina Piccola

Nestled on the eastern side of Sorrento, Marina Piccola is known for its stunning views of Mount Vesuvius and the Bay of Naples. This picturesque harbor is often bustling with activity as ferries and hydrofoils come and go. The waterfront is lined with vibrant cafes and restaurants, offering a perfect spot to relax and enjoy the maritime atmosphere.

- Marina Grande

Marina Grande, on the other hand, is the larger and more traditional of the two ports. It has a distinctively authentic feel with its colorful buildings and traditional fishing boats dotting the shoreline. The beach at Marina Grande is a favorite among locals and visitors alike, providing a tranquil setting to unwind after your sea voyage.

iv. Practical Tips for Sea Travel

- Check Schedules: Ferry and hydrofoil schedules can vary, especially during different seasons. It's advisable to check the current schedules and book tickets in advance, particularly if you're traveling during peak tourist times.

- Weather Considerations: The Tyrrhenian Sea can be calm and serene, but it's always wise to consider the weather conditions, especially if you're prone to seasickness. Checking the weather forecast before your sea journey ensures a smoother and more enjoyable experience.

- Port Facilities: Both Marina Piccola and Marina Grande offer essential facilities such as ticket counters, waiting areas, and information centers. Familiarize yourself with these facilities to make your transition from sea to land seamless.

- Transportation from Ports: Depending on your accommodation location, have a plan for transportation from the ports to your hotel. Taxis, buses, or even a short walk may be options, and it's beneficial to know what works best for you.

Sorrento's connection to the sea is not just a means of arriving but an introduction to the coastal allure that defines this enchanting town. Whether you choose the unhurried pace of a ferry or the swift glide of a hydrofoil, your arrival in Sorrento by sea promises to be a memorable prelude to the wonders that await on land.

2. Getting Around Sorrento

a. Walking

Sorrento's allure lies not only in its breathtaking vistas but also in the intimate embrace of its compact streets. Wandering through the heart of Sorrento, you'll find an enchanting labyrinth of cobblestone paths lined with vibrant bougainvillea and adorned with traditional architecture. The town's small size makes it a haven for pedestrians, inviting you to immerse yourself in the rich tapestry of local life.

As you stroll through Sorrento's streets, you'll discover a myriad of hidden gems—quaint cafes where the aroma of freshly brewed espresso wafts through the air, inviting you to indulge in a leisurely moment of people-watching. Charming boutiques beckon with handmade crafts and local treasures, providing a perfect opportunity to pick up a unique souvenir or two.

The beauty of Sorrento's pedestrian-friendly layout is not only in the ease of access to key attractions but also in the unhurried pace it encourages. Unlike bustling metropolises, Sorrento's streets invite you to meander without a set agenda, allowing serendipity to guide your journey. Perhaps you'll stumble upon a lively local market, where vendors proudly display an array of fresh produce and handmade goods, offering a glimpse into the authentic flavors of the region.

Sorrento's historic sites are seamlessly woven into the fabric of its pedestrian pathways. The Chiesa di San Francesco, with its intricately detailed facade, and the Basilica di Sant'Antonino, a testament to centuries of architectural grandeur, stand as silent witnesses to the town's storied past. The lack of vehicular traffic allows for a more profound connection with these landmarks, as you absorb the nuances of their design and the echoes of history that resonate within their walls.

As evening descends, the streets take on a magical quality, illuminated by the warm glow of street lamps and the twinkle of stars overhead. Sorrento's evenings are best enjoyed with a leisurely passeggiata, a traditional Italian evening stroll. Joining the locals in this timeless ritual, you'll feel the heartbeat of the town as it comes alive with the buzz of conversations and the strains of live music drifting from charming cafes.

The pedestrian-friendly nature of Sorrento is not just a logistical convenience; it's an invitation to savor every moment. Take the time to pause on a sun-dappled bench in a quiet piazza, sipping on a limoncello as you watch the world go by. The absence of the hum of engines allows for a symphony of sounds—the laughter of children playing, the melodies of street musicians, and the gentle lapping of waves against the nearby cliffs.

b. Local Buses

Sorrento boasts an efficient and extensive bus network that seamlessly weaves through the town's narrow streets and extends into the surrounding areas. These buses serve as lifelines, connecting not only the major attractions within Sorrento but also providing a gateway to the spectacular Amalfi Coast and the historic ruins of Pompeii.

The bus system in Sorrento is a testament to the town's commitment to providing accessible and affordable transportation options for both locals and visitors. The network is well-planned, ensuring that even the more remote corners of the region are within reach. As you board these buses, you'll find yourself immersed in the daily rhythm of Sorrentine life, with locals commuting alongside you, creating an authentic and communal travel experience.

One of the key advantages of relying on buses is the cost-effectiveness they offer. Compared to private transportation options, buses are a budget-friendly alternative, allowing you to allocate more of your travel budget to experiences, cuisine, and cultural exploration. This affordability makes them an attractive choice for those looking to maximize their stay without compromising on the richness of their travel experiences.

Whether you're planning a leisurely day exploring the charming streets of Sorrento or embarking on a more extensive journey to the Amalfi Coast or Pompeii, the bus system caters to various travel preferences. The convenience of hopping on a bus and being effortlessly transported to iconic destinations eliminates the stress of navigating unfamiliar roads or worrying about parking, allowing you to fully immerse yourself in the beauty and history that surrounds you.

Additionally, the bus routes are strategically designed to showcase the breathtaking landscapes that characterize the Amalfi Coast. As you wind along the cliffside roads, each twist and turn reveals postcard-perfect views of the azure Tyrrhenian Sea, quaint villages perched on hillsides, and lush, verdant landscapes. The journey itself becomes an integral part of the adventure, turning a simple commute into a scenic exploration that enriches your overall travel experience.

For those planning day trips to Pompeii, the bus system provides a hassle-free solution. Imagine stepping off the bus and into the ancient world of Pompeii, where centuries-old ruins come to life. The convenience of direct routes from Sorrento to Pompeii allows you to optimize your time at this archaeological marvel, delving into its history and marveling at the remarkably preserved remnants of a bygone era.

c. Renting a Scooter or Car

Renting a scooter or car in Sorrento opens up a world of possibilities for travelers seeking an immersive and personalized experience. The decision to opt for a scooter or car goes beyond mere convenience—it's about embracing the freedom to explore at your own pace, uncovering the lesser-known treasures that lie beyond the well-trodden tourist routes.

Imagine the wind in your hair as you navigate the winding roads that hug the rugged coastline. Sorrento, situated on the Sorrentine Peninsula, is surrounded by stunning landscapes, and a scooter or car rental allows you to dive deep into its beauty. As you drive along the cliffside roads, each turn reveals a new panorama of the azure Tyrrhenian Sea and the lush greenery that blankets the hills.

The allure of renting a scooter lies in the thrill of zipping through narrow streets and alleys that larger vehicles might struggle to traverse. It's an intimate way to connect with the local environment, as the sounds and scents of Sorrento envelop you. Parking becomes a breeze, with scooters fitting snugly into spaces that cars might find challenging.

For those with an adventurous spirit, renting a car provides a similar sense of autonomy but with added comfort and space. You can embark on day trips to neighboring towns and attractions, each offering its own unique charm. Picture yourself driving along the Amalfi Coast, the sheer cliffs on one side and the endless expanse of the sea on the other. With a car, you can stop at quaint villages, hidden beaches, and panoramic viewpoints, capturing the essence of the Sorrentine Peninsula in every moment.

Moreover, having a car at your disposal allows for spontaneous detours and exploration. Maybe you catch a glimpse of a sign pointing to a secluded cove or a centuries-old lemon grove. With the freedom that a car rental provides, you can follow these whims and discover the authentic, off-the-beaten-path gems that define the true spirit of Sorrento.

It's important to note that while renting a scooter or car offers unparalleled freedom, it also comes with responsibilities. Familiarize yourself with local traffic rules, ensure you have the necessary licenses, and drive with care, especially on the narrow and winding coastal roads. Additionally, be mindful of parking regulations in Sorrento, as the town can get quite congested during peak tourist seasons.

i. Parking

While renting a car offers convenience, parking in Sorrento can be challenging. It's advisable to inquire about parking facilities at your accommodation or use public parking lots on the outskirts of the town.

d. Taxis

When it comes to exploring Sorrento with ease and comfort, taxis stand out as a reliable and convenient mode of transportation. Whether you're arriving at the airport, your hotel, or any other point in the town, taxis are readily available to take you where you need to go.

Sorrento's taxi services are known for their efficiency and accessibility. You'll find taxi stands at key locations throughout the town, including popular landmarks, transportation hubs, and major hotels. If you're not near a taxi stand, your accommodation can assist in calling a taxi for you.

One of the conveniences of opting for a taxi is the door-to-door service it provides. This is especially advantageous if you have luggage, are traveling with family, or simply want a hassle-free journey from one point to another. Taxis offer a level of comfort and privacy that can be appealing, ensuring a smooth and stress-free experience during your stay in Sorrento.

However, it's crucial to be mindful of a few considerations when taking a taxi in Sorrento. Firstly, it's advisable to confirm whether the taxi has a functioning meter. The meter ensures a fair and transparent calculation of the fare based on the distance traveled. In the absence of a meter, it's essential to agree on the fare with the driver before embarking on your journey. This helps prevent any misunderstandings or disputes at the end of the ride.

In Sorrento, taxi drivers are generally friendly and accustomed to dealing with tourists. Don't hesitate to ask for recommendations or tips about the local attractions—they often have valuable insights that can enhance your overall experience. Additionally, most taxi drivers in Sorrento have a good understanding of English, making communication relatively straightforward for international visitors.

While taxis provide a level of convenience, it's important to note that they can be relatively more expensive compared to other modes of transportation, such as buses or walking. Therefore, it's a good idea to consider your budget and travel preferences when deciding on the most suitable transportation option for your needs.

4. Tips for Smooth Transportation

a. Plan Ahead

Before embarking on your journey, plan your transportation options based on your itinerary. Check schedules for buses, trains, and ferries, especially for day trips and excursions.

b. Purchase Transportation Passes

If you plan to use public transportation frequently, consider purchasing transportation passes for buses or trains. These passes often provide cost savings for multiple journeys.

c. Be Mindful of Peak Times

Sorrento, especially during the peak tourist season, can experience heavy traffic. Plan your transportation during off-peak hours to avoid delays.

d. Stay Informed about Strikes

Transportation strikes can occur in Italy. Stay informed about any planned strikes that might affect your travel plans, and have alternative arrangements in place.

Navigating Sorrento and its surroundings is an integral part of the travel experience. Whether you prefer the convenience of taxis, the freedom of renting a car, or the charm of walking through cobblestone streets, Sorrento offers a myriad of transportation options to suit every traveler's preferences. By planning ahead and exploring the various modes of transportation, you can make the most of your visit to this captivating destination on the Amalfi Coast.

Money Matters and Currency Exchange

As you plan your visit to this charming locale, it's essential to understand the nuances of money matters and currency exchange to make the most of your experience. we will walk you through the intricacies of Sorrento's currency, banking options, and provide tips on managing your finances during your stay.

The Currency: Euro (EUR)

Italy, like many other European countries, uses the Euro as its official currency. The Euro is denoted by the symbol € and is abbreviated as EUR. It is the second most traded currency in the world, making it crucial for visitors to familiarize themselves with its denominations and coins.

Denominations

- Banknotes: Euros come in various denominations of banknotes, including €5, €10, €20, €50, €100, €200, and €500. It's advisable to carry a mix of notes for different expenses.

- Coins: Coins are available in values of €1 and €2, as well as 1, 2, 5, 10, 20, and 50 cents. Having a coin purse will be convenient for smaller transactions.

Currency Exchange

Where to Exchange Currency

- Banks: Sorrento has several banks that offer currency exchange services. Banks usually provide competitive rates, and it's recommended to exchange a significant amount at once to minimize transaction fees.

- Exchange Bureaus: Exchange bureaus, often located in tourist areas, are another option. While convenient, be cautious of higher fees and less favorable exchange rates at these locations.

- ATMs: Using ATMs is a convenient way to obtain Euros. They are widely available in Sorrento, and you'll find them in banks, on the streets, and near popular tourist spots. Check with your home bank about international withdrawal fees to make an informed decision.

Exchange Rates

Exchange rates can fluctuate, impacting the amount of Euros you receive for your home currency. Stay updated on the current exchange rates before your trip, and consider using reliable currency converter apps for real-time information.

Banking in Sorrento

Understanding the local banking system is crucial for a smooth financial experience during your visit.

Banking Hours

Typically, banks in Sorrento are open from Monday to Friday, with operating hours ranging from 8:30 am to 1:30 pm. Some banks may reopen for a brief period in the afternoon, while others close for the day. Plan your banking activities accordingly.

Credit and Debit Cards

Credit and debit cards are widely accepted in Sorrento, especially in hotels, restaurants, and larger shops. However, it's advisable to carry some cash, particularly for smaller establishments or places that may not accept cards. Notify your bank of your travel dates to avoid any potential issues with card transactions.

Currency Conversion Fees

While using your credit card can be convenient, be aware of currency conversion fees that may apply. Some credit cards offer more favorable terms for international transactions, so check with your card provider to understand the fees involved.

Money Management Tips

Budgeting

Create a budget for your Sorrento trip to manage your expenses effectively. Factor in accommodation, meals, transportation, and activities. Having a clear budget will help you allocate your funds wisely.

Emergency Funds

It's always a good idea to have some emergency funds in a secure location, such as a money belt or a hidden pocket in your bag. This ensures you have a backup in case of unforeseen circumstances.

Local Spending Habits

Understanding local spending habits can help you gauge how much cash you'll need on a daily basis. For instance, if you plan to explore local markets or small shops, having some cash on hand is essential.

Familiarize yourself with the Euro, choose the right method for currency exchange, and embrace the convenience of card payments while keeping some cash for those charming local experiences. By following these tips, you'll be well-equipped to enjoy your Sorrento adventure without any financial hiccups.

Health Precautions

Whether you're exploring the charming streets, indulging in delicious local cuisine, or relaxing on the beautiful beaches, it's essential to prioritize your health and well-being during your visit. we'll outline key health precautions to ensure a safe and enjoyable experience in Sorrento.

1. Understanding Local Health Infrastructure

Before embarking on your journey, it's crucial to familiarize yourself with the local health infrastructure in Sorrento. Identify the location of hospitals, clinics, and pharmacies, ensuring you have access to medical assistance if needed. Additionally, research local emergency contact numbers, including the nearest embassy or consulate.

2. Travel Insurance: A Must-Have

Investing in comprehensive travel insurance is a non-negotiable aspect of any trip. Ensure that your insurance covers medical emergencies, trip cancellations, and unexpected events. Keep a copy of your insurance policy and emergency contact information with you at all times.

3. Stay Hydrated and Maintain a Healthy Diet

Sorrento's Mediterranean climate can be warm, especially during the summer months. Stay hydrated by drinking plenty of water throughout the day, and incorporate local fruits and vegetables into your diet. This not only supports your overall well-being but also enhances your travel experience by indulging in the region's culinary delights.

4. Sun Protection is Key

The sun in Sorrento can be intense, so sun protection is paramount. Pack and regularly apply a high SPF sunscreen, wear a wide-brimmed hat, and use sunglasses to shield your eyes. Avoid prolonged exposure during peak sunlight hours, typically from 10 a.m. to 4 p.m.

5. Adapting to the Local Pace

Sorrento is known for its relaxed pace of life. Embrace this by allowing yourself to unwind and take breaks when needed. Overexertion can lead to fatigue and stress, impacting your overall well-being. Take leisurely strolls, enjoy the local cafés, and savor the beauty of the surroundings at a comfortable pace.

6. Local Cuisine Considerations

Sorrento is a haven for food enthusiasts, offering a variety of culinary delights. However, if you have dietary restrictions or allergies, communicate these clearly when dining out. Familiarize yourself with common ingredients in local dishes to avoid any potential health issues.

7. Stay Informed About Water Safety

If you plan to indulge in Sorrento's beautiful coastal offerings, be mindful of water safety. Pay attention to local advisories, follow designated swimming areas, and be cautious of strong currents. If you're participating in water activities, ensure you have the necessary skills and equipment.

8. Footwear for Exploration

Sorrento's terrain can vary, from cobbled streets to uneven pathways. Choose comfortable footwear suitable for walking and exploration. This not only prevents discomfort but also reduces the risk of injuries while navigating different surfaces.

9. Mosquito Protection

During certain times of the year, mosquitoes can be prevalent. Pack insect repellent and consider wearing long sleeves and pants during evenings, especially if you plan to explore outdoor areas. This precaution helps protect against mosquito-borne illnesses.

10. Emergency First Aid Kit

Carry a basic first aid kit with essentials such as bandages, pain relievers, and any prescribed medications. While Sorrento has pharmacies, having a small kit on hand ensures quick access to basic medical supplies.

11. Local Healthcare Customs

Familiarize yourself with local healthcare customs and practices. In Sorrento, as in many parts of Italy, pharmacies play a crucial role in healthcare. Pharmacists can provide advice and over-the-counter medications, making it a good first point of contact for minor health concerns.

12. Respect Cultural Norms

Respecting local customs is not only a matter of etiquette but also contributes to your overall well-being. For example, in Sorrento, it's customary to greet people with a friendly "buongiorno" (good morning) or "buonasera" (good evening). Showing respect for local customs can enhance your experience and foster positive interactions.

13. Hygiene Practices

Maintaining good hygiene practices is fundamental to staying healthy during your visit. Wash your hands regularly, especially before meals, and carry hand sanitizer for situations where soap and water are not readily available.

14. Stay Active and Relaxed

Strike a balance between exploration and relaxation. Engage in activities that promote physical well-being, such as scenic walks, yoga, or swimming. Balancing activity with relaxation ensures you make the most of your time in Sorrento while taking care of your health.

Sorrento offers a magical blend of history, culture, and natural beauty. By prioritizing your health and following these precautions, you can fully immerse yourself in the wonders of this enchanting destination. Remember, a healthy traveler is a happy traveler, and Sorrento's charm is best enjoyed when you're at your best. Safe travels!

Emergency contact numbers

While you're bound to have a fantastic time exploring the historic sites, enjoying the local cuisine, and soaking in the sun along the Amalfi Coast, it's crucial to prioritize your safety. Accidents and emergencies can happen anywhere, and being prepared with the right emergency contact numbers is essential. we'll provide you with the necessary information to ensure a safe and secure visit to Sorrento.

General Emergency Numbers

1. Emergency Services (Police, Fire, Ambulance): 112

The universal emergency number in Italy, including Sorrento, is 112. This number connects you to the police, fire brigade, and medical emergency services. It is important to note that English-speaking operators are available to assist you.

2. Medical Emergency (Ambulance): 118

If you or someone you are with requires immediate medical attention, dial 118 to request an ambulance. Provide clear information about the situation and your location to ensure a swift response from medical professionals.

3. Police: 113

For non-emergency police assistance or to report a crime, dial 113. The local police in Sorrento are trained to handle various situations and can provide assistance in English.

Healthcare Services

4. Sorrento Hospital (Ospedale di Sorrento): +39 081 878 81 11

In case of serious medical issues, Sorrento has a local hospital equipped to handle emergencies. The Sorrento Hospital provides a range of medical services, and the staff is accustomed to dealing with international visitors.

5. Pharmacies (Farmacie)

Pharmacies in Sorrento play a crucial role in providing over-the-counter medications and health advice. In case you need medication or assistance for a minor ailment, you can locate the nearest pharmacy. Note that pharmacies operate on a rotating schedule for after-hours service, so it's essential to check the sign on the pharmacy door for the one open in the evening.

Tourist Assistance

6. Tourist Police: +39 081 807 10 11

Sorrento, being a popular tourist destination, has a dedicated Tourist Police service to assist visitors. If you encounter any issues or need information related to tourism, don't hesitate to contact the Tourist Police.

7. Emergency Consular Assistance

For citizens of foreign countries, it's wise to have your embassy or consulate's contact information on hand. They can provide assistance with lost passports, legal issues, and other consular services.

Transportation Emergencies

8. Roadside Assistance: 803 116

If you're renting a car and encounter any issues on the road, such as a breakdown or accident, you can call the dedicated roadside assistance number. They can provide support and arrange for necessary services.

9. Public Transportation: +39 081 763 16 60

For emergencies related to public transportation, including buses and trains, you can contact the local transportation authority. They can assist with issues such as lost items or disruptions in service.

Natural Disasters

10. Civil Protection: 800 840 840

Italy, including Sorrento, is prone to occasional seismic activity. While the chances of a significant earthquake during your visit are low, it's good to be prepared. The Civil Protection number can provide information and guidance in case of natural disasters.

Additional Tips for a Safe Visit

- Travel Insurance: Before embarking on your trip to Sorrento, consider purchasing travel insurance. This can provide coverage for medical emergencies, trip cancellations, and other unforeseen events.

- Local Emergency Information: Upon arrival in Sorrento, familiarize yourself with the location of the nearest hospital, pharmacy, and police station. Having this information readily available can save crucial time in case of an emergency.

- Language Assistance: While English is widely spoken in tourist areas, it's beneficial to learn a few basic Italian phrases related to emergencies. This can help in communicating effectively in case you encounter someone who doesn't speak English.

- Emergency Kit: Pack a small emergency kit with essential items such as a first aid kit, prescription medications, a flashlight, and a list of important contacts.

By being proactive and aware of the emergency contact numbers in Sorrento, you are taking a significant step towards ensuring your safety during your visit. While emergencies are rare, having the right information at your fingertips can make a crucial difference. Enjoy your time in Sorrento, explore its beauty, and have peace of mind knowing that you are well-prepared for any unforeseen circumstances.

Tourist Traps to Avoid

like any popular tourist spot, Sorrento has its fair share of tourist traps that can hinder your experience. In this guide, we'll explore some common pitfalls and offer insights on how to avoid them, ensuring your visit is as enjoyable and authentic as possible.

1. Overpriced Waterfront Dining

The Trap:
One of the most common tourist traps in Sorrento is falling for the allure of waterfront dining without checking prices beforehand. While the views are undoubtedly stunning, some restaurants take advantage of their prime locations by charging exorbitant prices for mediocre food.

Avoidance Strategy:
Before choosing a waterfront restaurant, do some research on review sites or ask locals for recommendations. Look for places that strike a balance between good food and fair prices. Exploring the backstreets often leads to hidden gems that are more budget-friendly.

2. Aggressive Street Vendors

The Trap:
Sorrento, like many popular tourist destinations, has its fair share of street vendors selling souvenirs. While some are

genuine, others may use aggressive tactics to pressure you into buying overpriced items.
Avoidance Strategy:
Stay vigilant and politely decline persistent vendors. If you're interested in purchasing souvenirs, consider shopping at local markets where you can find authentic products at reasonable prices. Bargaining is common in these settings, so don't be afraid to negotiate.

3. Dubious Currency Exchange Services

The Trap:
Currency exchange booths near popular tourist attractions might offer convenience, but they often come with unfavorable exchange rates and hidden fees.

Avoidance Strategy:
Use ATMs or banks for currency exchange, and be aware of the current exchange rates before arriving. ATMs usually provide better rates, and withdrawing smaller amounts at a time can minimize fees. Avoid exchanging money at kiosks with rates that seem too good to be true.

4. Guided Tours with Hidden Fees

The Trap:
Some guided tours advertised as all-inclusive may have hidden fees that are only revealed once you're on the tour. These can include additional charges for entrance fees, transportation, or optional activities.

Avoidance Strategy:
Read the fine print before booking any guided tours. Look for reviews from other travelers to ensure transparency about additional costs. Alternatively, consider exploring

some attractions independently to save money and have a more personalized experience.

5. Taxis and Transportation Scams

The Trap:
Unscrupulous taxi drivers may take advantage of tourists by charging inflated fares or taking unnecessarily long routes to popular destinations.

Avoidance Strategy:
Research standard taxi fares in advance and agree on a price before starting your journey. Consider using reputable ride-sharing apps or public transportation for shorter distances. If you're unsure, ask locals for advice on fair transportation costs.

6. Fake Tourist Information Centers

The Trap:
Some areas may have unofficial tourist information centers that provide inaccurate or misleading information to steer tourists towards specific businesses.

Avoidance Strategy:
Rely on official tourist information centers or websites endorsed by the local tourism board. These sources are more likely to provide accurate information about attractions, events, and services.

7. Time-Share Presentations

The Trap:
Be wary of invitations to attend time-share presentations, often disguised as free tours or activities. These

presentations can be high-pressure sales pitches, and attendees may feel obligated to make a purchase.

Avoidance Strategy:
Politely decline invitations to time-share presentations and be cautious of offers that seem too good to be true. Focus on exploring the destination independently and seek recommendations from fellow travelers for genuine experiences.

8. Paying for Public Restrooms

The Trap:
In some tourist-heavy areas, you may encounter pay-per-use public restrooms. While this practice is not uncommon, the fees can be disproportionately high.

Avoidance Strategy:
Be prepared by carrying small denominations of local currency for restroom fees. Alternatively, use facilities in restaurants or cafes where restroom access is often free for customers.

9. Non-Official Tour Guides

The Trap:
Some individuals posing as tour guides may offer their services without official accreditation, leading to subpar experiences and potential safety concerns.

Avoidance Strategy:
Choose licensed tour guides recommended by reputable travel agencies or tourism boards. Official guides are knowledgeable about the destination, follow ethical practices, and prioritize the safety of their clients.

10. High-Pressure Photo Ops

The Trap:
Photographers at popular tourist spots may approach you for impromptu photo sessions, only to demand high fees for the pictures afterward.

Avoidance Strategy:
Politely decline offers from unsolicited photographers and rely on your own camera or smartphone for pictures. If you do want professional photos, research local photography services in advance and agree on prices before the session.

By staying informed and adopting a cautious approach, you can navigate Sorrento's tourist traps and enjoy an authentic and rewarding experience. Embrace the local culture, interact with locals, and explore beyond the well-trodden paths to discover the true charm of this enchanting destination. Sorrento has much to offer, and with a bit of savvy travel planning, you can make the most of your visit without falling into common tourist traps.

Conclusion

In conclusion, this Sorrento Travel Guide stands as a comprehensive and invaluable companion for anyone embarking on a journey to this mesmerizing destination. Throughout the pages, we have delved into the rich tapestry of Sorrento's cultural heritage, explored the breathtaking landscapes, and navigated the nuances of its vibrant community. As we bid farewell to the guide, it is evident that Sorrento is not merely a place on the map; it is an experience waiting to be embraced.

The guide has meticulously crafted a narrative that transcends the conventional boundaries of travel literature. It goes beyond the perfunctory listings of attractions and accommodations, offering readers an immersive exploration of the soul of Sorrento. By understanding the historical roots, cultural nuances, and the day-to-day life of the locals, the guide has transformed from a mere informational resource into a portal that transports readers into the heart of this enchanting Italian town.

One of the defining features of this guide is its commitment to ensuring a seamless and enriching travel experience. From the moment readers pick up the book to the time they bid arrivederci to Sorrento, every aspect of their journey is meticulously addressed. The practical tips on health precautions, emergency contact numbers, and local customs serve as a testament to the guide's dedication to the well-being and safety of its readers. In a world where travel can be unpredictable, having a reliable companion like this Sorrento Travel Guide becomes indispensable.

Beyond the factual information, the guide succeeds in painting a vivid and alluring picture of Sorrento. It captures the essence of the town in words, transporting readers to the sun-kissed cliffs overlooking the Bay of Naples, allowing them to savor the aroma of lemons in the air and feel the warmth of the Mediterranean sun on their skin. The guide is not just a manual; it is a storyteller, narrating the tale of Sorrento with passion and eloquence.

As we reflect on the journey through the guide, it becomes evident that Sorrento is not just a destination; it's an invitation to a transformative experience. It beckons travelers to immerse themselves in the local way of life, to savor the flavors of authentic Italian cuisine, and to forge connections with the welcoming inhabitants of this coastal haven. The guide serves as a bridge, connecting the reader to the heart and soul of Sorrento in a way that transcends the limitations of traditional travel literature.

Furthermore, the Sorrento Travel Guide is not a static entity. It evolves with the dynamic nature of travel, adapting to the changing needs and expectations of its readers. The inclusion of emergency contact numbers reflects a foresight into the unpredictable nature of life and travel. By equipping readers with the necessary tools to navigate unforeseen circumstances, the guide transcends its role as a mere informant and emerges as a reliable and caring companion.

In essence, the Sorrento Travel Guide extends an invitation to embark on a journey of discovery and self-renewal. It is a call to explore not just the geographical wonders of Sorrento but also the depths of one's own curiosity and wanderlust. As readers close the final pages of this guide, they are not just armed with information; they carry with them the spirit of Sorrento—the echoes of its history, the warmth of its people, and the promise of a transformative adventure.

In the grand tapestry of travel literature, this Sorrento Travel Guide stands as a masterpiece—a fusion of practicality and poetry, information and inspiration. Whether you are a seasoned traveler or a first-time explorer, this guide extends a hand, guiding you through the cobbled streets and hidden gems of Sorrento with grace and enthusiasm. As the saying goes, "To travel is to live," and with this Sorrento Travel Guide in hand, that journey becomes not just a passage of miles, but a profound and enriching chapter in the book of life. Buon viaggio!

Printed in Great Britain
by Amazon

38391611R00099